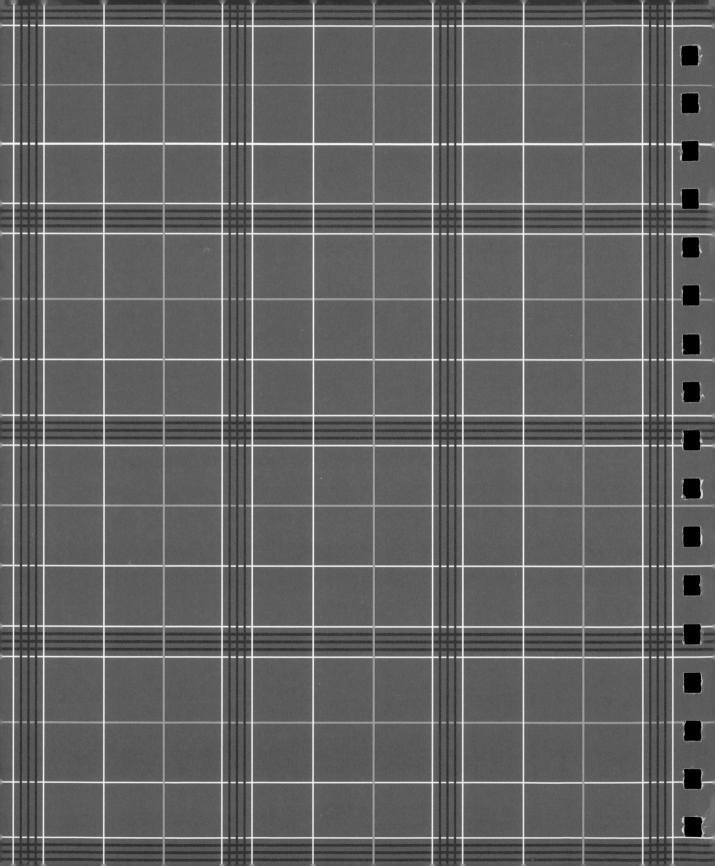

DECEPTIVELY DELICIOUS

Simple Secrets to Get Your Kids Eating Good Food

by Jessica Seinfeld

Photographs by **LISA HUBBARD** • Illustrations by **STEVE VANCE**

Design by **HEADCASE DESIGN**

Produced by

MELCHER MEDIA

Published by

Collins

An Imprint of HarperCollinsPublishers

HarperCollins books may be purchased for educational, business, or sales promotional use. For information please write: Special Markets Department, HarperCollins Publishers, 10 East 53rd Street, New York, NY 10022.

Photographs copyright © 2007 Lisa Hubbard
Illustrations copyright © 2007 Steve Vance

FIRST EDITION

This book was produced by

 MELCHER
MEDIA

124 West 13th Street • New York, NY 10011
www.melcher.com

Publisher: Charles Melcher • Associate Publisher: Bonnie Eldon
Editor in Chief: Duncan Bock • Senior Editor and Project Manager: Lia Ronnen
Assistant Editor: Lauren Nathan • Production Director: Kurt Andrews

Designed by Headcase Design
www.headcasedesign.com

Library of Congress Cataloging-in-Publication Data

Seinfeld, Jessica.
Deceptively delicious : simple secrets to get your kids eating good foods / Jessica Seinfeld ; photographs by Lisa Hubbard ; with illustrations by Steve Vance ; design by Headcase Design. — 1st ed.
p. cm.
Includes index.

ISBN 978-0-06-125134-4

1. Cookery, American. I. Title.

TX715.S145735 2007   641.5973--dc22

2007022217

07 08 09 10 11   10   9

To Jerry, Sascha, Julian, and Shepherd—
thank you for filling me up
with love every day.

—J.S.

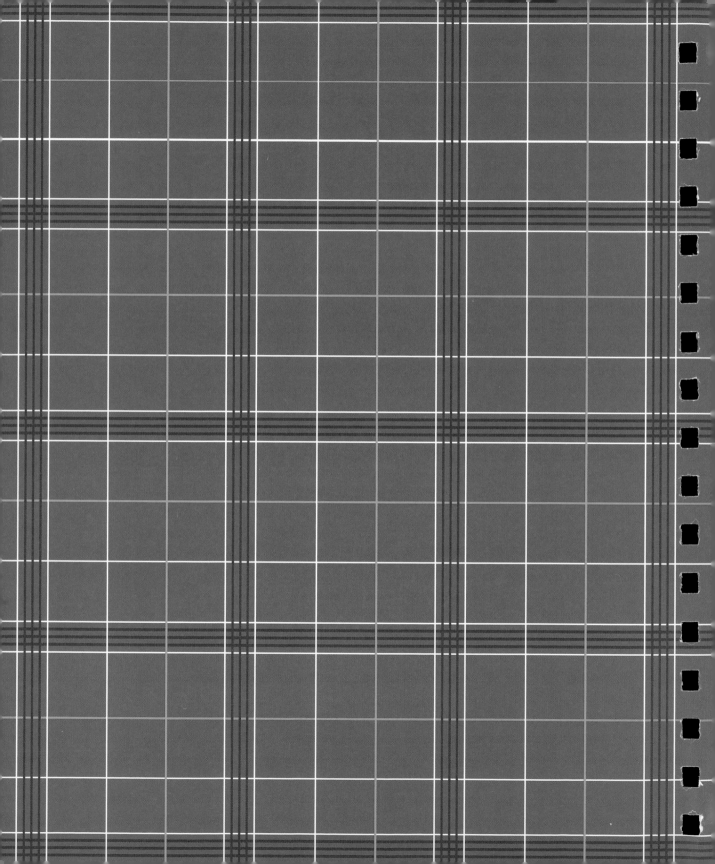

CONTENTS

Foreword
by Dr. Roxana Mehran and Dr. Mehmet Oz 8

Introduction 10

Changing Habits Through Loving Deception 13

Meet the Kitchen Cabinet 14

The Program 16
    • Equip Your Kitchen 18
    • Stock Your Pantry 22
    • The Purees: How-To 24
        • *Vegetable Purees* 28
        • *Fruit Purees* 30
    • The Basics: Cooking Rice, Pasta, Chicken, and Beef 31

What Every Parent Should Know About Nutrition
by Joy Bauer 32
    • Easy Nutritional Guidelines for Children 34
    • What's in that Veggie? 37
    • What's in that Fruit? 40

The Recipes 43
    • Breakfast Recipes 47
    • Mealtime Recipes 71
    • Dessert Recipes 155

Appendix: The ABCs of Nutrition 202

Index 205

Acknowledgments 208

FOREWORD

By Dr. Roxana Mehran and Dr. Mehmet Oz

IT IS 7 A.M. and I am almost late for my early morning meeting at the hospital, but I am also concerned about getting my three girls ready for school and making sure their first meal of the day—breakfast—is a healthy one. Are they getting enough fiber and vitamins? Is there too much fat or sugar in their food? Later that morning, as I see my first patient, a thirty-five-year-old obese diabetic who is about to undergo a procedure to open blocked arteries, I am reminded of how important it is to protect my young girls from heart disease.

My colleague and friend, Dr. Mehmet Oz, a heart surgeon at Columbia University and a longtime advocate for healthy living—as well as a father of four—has the same concerns for his family. As physicians who care for heart disease patients, we have witnessed and treated too many young patients with early blockages of the arteries.

Our heart disease patients are heavier, and also younger, than they have ever been. This pattern is disturbing, and our children are at risk of living shorter lives than their parents. We know that this disease is largely preventable through a healthful diet and as doctors, it is our job to educate and teach our patients ways to improve their lives. As parents, we know how important it is to teach our children good habits early on.

Ironically, most people are actually aware of the fundamentals of a healthy diet and the necessity of eating more vegetables and fruits while avoiding too much starch, sugar, and saturated fat. Yet having fruits and vegetables every day

Beets   Broccoli   Carrots   Avocado   Blueberries   Prunes   Spinach   Squash   Sweet Potatoes   Zucchini

and breaking long-standing dietary habits seem to be the greatest challenges people face.

The fact is that the consumption of vegetables is the cornerstone of any diet, be it cardiovascular, diabetic, or weight loss. While it's the basis of vegetarian diets, as well as Mediterranean and other region-specific diets, it is not a part of our national way of eating. That's unfortunate: vegetables and fruits contain many vitamins, minerals, and fiber—nutrients that strengthen our bodies and help them grow in a healthy way.

We've all had the experience of arguing with our children over eating their vegetables, and the resulting frustration is enough to make us want to give up altogether. That's where *Deceptively Delicious* comes in. These wonderful recipes introduce our children's taste buds to the good, healthy foods, but kids still get to eat the foods they love. Later, as they grow, they will want healthy vegetables on their own, since, for years, they had their chicken nuggets coated with them already!

Jessica Seinfeld addresses the heart of the problem: its practical implementation. She simplifies the dilemma of how to start by telling us exactly which kitchen supplies we need and showing us tricks for preparing meals simply and efficiently. Daily routines are not disturbed, while the dedicated time for this effort is minimized. It is clear to us that the benefits clearly outweigh the work that goes into feeding your family.

This book is an innovative approach to feeding our children healthful foods at an early age without added stress for either parents or children. It also speaks for the quest of a dedicated mother: the author. She has explored every possible solution in order to do the right thing for her family, and she felt compelled to share her rewarding findings with the world. She has done all the work, and now we can benefit from her efforts. Her simple, practical idea—and its effective implementation—impressed us. We hope many other parents will read this book and take its information to heart when cooking family meals.

Navy Beans *Artichoke* *Pineapples* *Mushrooms* *Raspberries* *Pumpkins* *Cherries* *Cauliflower* *Peppers* *Chickpeas*

INTRODUCTION

I had begun to dread mealtime.

I had tried everything, and yet all my efforts to feed my family were being undermined by a powerful force: vegetables. Mealtimes were reduced to a constant pushing and pulling, with me forever begging my kids to eat their vegetables, and them protesting unhappily. Instead of laughing and having fun with my family, I was irritated and stressed as I labored to coerce them to eat food they found "disgusting." I couldn't take it anymore. I just wanted a little peace around the dinner table.

Then, one evening while I was cooking dinner, pureeing butternut squash for the baby and making mac and cheese for the rest of us, I had the crazy idea of stirring a little of the puree into the macaroni. And so I did. The colors matched—you couldn't really see the squash in there—and the tex-ture was perfect. So I stirred in a little more, tasting to make sure the flavor of the squash didn't overpower the cheese. Feeling only a little guilty that I was tricking my children, I stirred in enough of the squash to feel satisfied that I was giving them a respectable portion of vegetables.

And then I held my breath.

It worked! The kids, entirely innocent of my deceit, plowed happily through their dinners. I was beside myself with joy. I couldn't stop smiling at the knowledge that my kids had eaten vegetables without a word from me. My husband, Jerry, was dying to know what all my smiling was about. It was the first meal in a very long time during which I hadn't said, "Eat your vegetables," even once. And that was pure pleasure.

I have not uttered the dreaded phrase since and from that meal on, I have become an expert at hiding vegetable purees and other healthful additions—foods my kids wouldn't touch otherwise—in all of their favorite dishes. The whole family is happier, and we can finally enjoy mealtimes again.

Since becoming a mom, I've discovered that being a parent is largely about being challenged *all the time*. Whether you work outside the home or stay at home with your children, parenting is just plain difficult, and mealtimes are often an unpleasant pressure point. All we want is to make simple, fast, nutritious meals that our kids will actually eat. But after just one experience of watching a child throw our best efforts onto the floor, or refuse to eat, we just want to give up. Who has that kind of time—and food—to waste?

The recipes in *Deceptively Delicious* changed that equation for me.

This book is nothing more than one mom's coping skills. We all have shortcuts and wisdom we learn from our own mothers, from friends, and from the best teacher of all—failure. But there's no reason why everyone has to repeat the same mistakes. You should know that for every recipe in this book, I've tried ten others that no one—and I mean *no one*—liked. I've endured the catastrophes so you don't have to.

I'm not a professional chef—far from it—and these recipes require no training or kitchen knowledge whatsoever. Each one has been tested—relentlessly—on my own kids and other families with young children. And when I found the gems that worked for me, I enlisted the help of a wonderful kid-friendly chef, Jennifer Iserloh, to distill my research into practical recipes any family can enjoy.

I've chosen dishes that I'm confident children and parents will feel comfortable with because they're the familiar ones that kids love already—macaroni and cheese, tacos, chicken nuggets, pizza, pancakes, and brownies. The recipes were developed for speed and ease, and most of them are doable in thirty minutes or less, with only five to twenty minutes of actual work. (Total cooking time, as well as prep time, are listed at the top of each recipe.) And they all conform to nutrition expert Joy Bauer's rigorous standards of nutrition.

But if there's one thing I've learned both from cooking these recipes, and from having three strong-willed children, it is this: ensuring your family's nutrition requires much more than just the ability to follow a recipe. To make every meal (or nearly every meal) a healthful one, you need a system that works for your family's lifestyle.

So, in addition to the simple, family-friendly meals contained in here, you'll also find tips and suggestions from other parents with young children that could inspire and help you in your *own* home.

Organization is key: being prepared makes the most of your precious time and will give you the confidence to cook. So before you even get to the recipes, I've laid out a strategy for gathering a collection of must-have kitchen utensils; stocking your kitchen pantry so that you always have staple ingredients on hand; and, of course, making the purees. Once you've got your kitchen in order, you'll find that cooking is the fun and easy part.

I've also gotten advice from two parenting experts, Jean Mandelbaum and Pat Shimm; and I've included their wisdom in the book as a series of tips running throughout. You'll see that I'm the sort of mom who likes rules—I work best with structure—so I'm giving you the rules that I use in my household. It's what works for me, but, of course, the best methods are the ones that work for you and your family.

The day that Jerry and I came home from the hospital with our first child, Sascha, we looked at each other and said, "Okay, now what?" We had no idea what we were doing—we were so clueless. We couldn't believe they let us leave with her! But there's no recipe to parenting, and I've spent every day of the ensuing six years just trying to figure it all out, solving problems and putting out fires. I find that these days I actually enjoy the process of solving parenting problems—I don't mind failing now and then until I find a better way.

I hope that this book will give you the same confidence, or at least, ensure that you never again have to hear yourself say, "Eat your vegetables!" But more than anything, I hope *Deceptively Delicious* will give you the tools you need to give your family good, healthful, and peaceful meals.

CHANGING HABITS THROUGH LOVING DECEPTION

WOULDN'T IT BE great if kids came into the world with the innate desire to eat the right foods?

In reality, however, too many food choices—many of them unhealthy—make it impossible for kids to distinguish the good from the bad. It's up to us as parents to make choices for them, at least until they are able to figure things out for themselves.

And it's not realistic to simply disregard their food aversions, either. Forcing your kids to eat foods they hate only reinforces their distaste.

That's where a little loving deception comes in handy. *Deceptively Delicious* enables parents to give kids what they want and what they need at the same time. It acknowledges your kids' genuine dislikes without being confined by them. It empowers you to exert some legitimate control over what your children eat, without inviting the usual fights. And most important, it's a way to give your kids a head start toward eating what's good for them so that they'll grow up and eat better food throughout their lives.

Just as the most powerful lessons are the ones that aren't taught, the best parenting solutions are the ones that build good habits—invisibly. I want my kids to associate food and mealtimes with happiness and conversation, not power struggles and strife. With a little sleight of hand, you can make the issue of what your children will and will not eat disappear from the table.

Meet the
KITCHEN CABINET

Jessica

    Hi, I'm **JESSICA**, and this is my Kitchen Cabinet, my all-important staff of advisors. My three children are my official recipe tasters. They are my toughest critics. If they approve, I am confident that your tasters will too. I've also tried these recipes out on their little friends and cousins who come by the house, some of whom are difficult eaters as well.

Sascha

SASCHA, our oldest, is six years old, and she is my toughest taster. In fact, she is practically impossible to please. From birth, it seems, she has been decisively clear about what she will and won't eat. She takes a hesitant and apprehensive approach to food and rarely will try anything new. Sweets are the exception, however, and she will try anything that even remotely looks like dessert.

Julian

JULIAN, our middle child, is four years old. He's a good eater if his older sister isn't around to influence him. On his own, he's happy to eat what is presented to him, but when he's with Sascha, he falls prey to whatever she dictates. So all of a sudden, even when I've cooked food I know he likes, he's pushing his plate away and saying, "I don't like it." And now I've got not one, but two kids who aren't eating, and with whom I would have spent the rest of the meal negotiating.

Shepherd

SHEPHERD, our "baby," is two years old, and he is a remarkable eater. He will eat anything. ANYTHING. He will eat himself sick. The first word he spoke was "that," which was baby talk for "I want THAT food, there, on your plate."

Jerry

My husband, **JERRY**, is a great eater. He's quite happy to eat vegetables and any healthy food I make, for that matter. In fact, he'll pretty much go along with whatever's happening, which is one of the many things that make him such a great husband. And he's a marvelous taster because, unlike the kids, he'll say things other than, "Ew, gross, this is disgusting."

THE PROGRAM

Getting organized will make your life much easier. Follow these four steps to healthful family meals.

①	②	③	④
Equip your kitchen with tools that make cooking easier. (page 18)	*Stock your kitchen with staple ingredients that you will use again and again.* (page 22)	*Make purees, a few at a time, and then portion and freeze them for use in the recipes.* (page 24)	*The recipes. The deception begins!* (page 43)

If you've read this far, you're ready for action. So here's my plan.

To encourage your family to eat better, you'll need to make a few changes in the way you cook. The first step is to put together a number of simple fruit and vegetable purees. You will quickly and easily learn to prepare, cook, puree, and portion the purees. Then the purees will be available to use when they're called for, just like any other ingredient in my recipes.

I learned from changing my own cooking habits that I needed to recalibrate my brain—I needed a systematic approach to organize myself. And I'm going to show you my system so that you can set things up in your own home to make cooking as efficient as possible.

Theoretically, you can make a puree as you need it, that is, just before you make the recipe in which it's used. I can tell you, though, that it doesn't work that way in my house. If I can reach into my freezer and grab a portion of butternut squash, my kids will be eating mac and cheese twenty minutes later, whether I've added the squash to my own recipe or to a packaged mix. If the squash isn't there, it's back to "Eat your vegetables" for me.

Think of me as your kitchen trainer. I want to encourage you to spend about an hour each week preparing the purees so that you'll always have them on hand. You certainly won't *want* to do it every week (how much do you really want to go to the gym?) but you'll find that it's worth it. As change begins to happen, you'll hardly notice the extra 2–5 minutes it takes to puree, and you'll increasingly find nooks of time to do it. Pureeing will become a habit, like anything else.

EQUIP YOUR KITCHEN

There are a few pieces of special equipment that will help you to become an efficient and accomplished chef de puree.

It's useful to have both a large piece of equipment (such as a standard-sized food processor or blender) and a smaller one (such as a mini food processor or Magic Bullet); the food processor is best for making a large quantity of purees, but if you find yourself pureeing for just one dish, a mini-chopper is better.

FOR STEAMING	FOR PUREEING
Rice steamer, collapsible steamer, or pasta pot with a drainer basket	*Food processor, Magic Bullet, or blender for pureeing and chopping*

Of the three, my favorite is a **rice steamer**, because I can set the timer and the steamer turns off automatically. I can go off and do things around the house, and the buzzer calls me back to the kitchen when the vegetables are done.

Some people like to use a blender, but I prefer a **food processor** or **Magic Bullet** (my husband actually bought this from a late-night television promotion and I love it) for chopping and pureeing because the purees come out a little smoother.

FOR THE PUREES

Strainer or colander

Cutting board

Vegetable peeler

Large (10-inch) chef's knife

Small paring knife

1- and 2-quart saucepans

6- and 8-quart pots

Kitchen timer

Wooden spoons: small, medium, and large

Measuring cup and spoon

Food storage bags

Black permanent marker to label the puree bags

OTHER HELPFUL COOKING TOOLS

Plastic storage bins	*Scissors (to snip open zipper-lock bags of puree)*	*Box grater*
		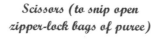
Waxed paper, aluminum foil, and cooking parchment	*Potato ricer or potato masher*	*Large (12-inch) nonstick skillet and large ovenproof nonstick skillet*

Baking dishes	*Popsicle mold (2-ounce popsicles)*	*9x5-inch loaf pan*

FOR BAKING

| Heatproof silicone spatula | Whisk | Mixing bowls |

| Ice cream scoop for filling muffin cups | 12-cup muffin pan; mini-muffin pan or doughnut mold | Large baking sheets |

| Baking pans (8x8-inch and 9x12-inch) | Cooling rack | 9-inch cake pan |

| 9-inch pie plate | Electric mixer (optional, but great to have) | Paper baking cups |

② STOCK YOUR PANTRY

PERISHABLES

- Large eggs
- Trans-fat-free soft tub margarine spread
- Reduced-fat sour cream
- Lowfat plain or Greek yogurt

- Reduced-fat mayonnaise
- Reduced-fat mozzarella and Cheddar cheeses
- Parmesan
- Lowfat (1%) buttermilk

- Reduced-fat cream cheese
- Reduced-fat cottage cheese
- Nonfat (skim) milk
- Wheat germ
- Flaxseed meal

SPICES

- Salt
- Fresh ground pepper
- Allspice
- Dried basil
- Chili powder

- Cinnamon
- Ground cloves
- Ground cumin
- Garlic powder
- Whole or ground nutmeg

- Onion powder
- Sweet paprika
- Pumpkin pie spice
- Dried thyme

GRAINS AND SUCH

- Whole-wheat bread
- Brown rice
- Couscous
- Pastas (preferably whole-grain or multi-grain)

such as penne, elbows, alphabet, and spaghetti
- No-boil lasagna noodles
- Whole-wheat tortillas

FOR BAKING

- Whole-wheat flour
- All-purpose flour
- Oatmeal—old-fashioned and quick-cooking oats
- Granulated sugar
- Confectioners' sugar

- Light and dark brown sugar
- Semisweet or bittersweet baking chocolate
- Semisweet chocolate chips
- Unsweetened cocoa powder
- Molasses
- Pure vanilla extract
- Pure lemon extract
- Natural applesauce
- Dried apricots, prunes, and cherries

- Chopped pecans and walnuts
- Cornstarch
- Canola or vegetable oil
- Baking soda
- Baking powder
- Cake mixes (yellow, devil's food, and brownie)
- Instant pancake mix
- Lowfat graham crackers
- Marshmallows

IN THE CUPBOARD

- Olive oil
- Nonstick cooking spray
- Natural peanut butter (I love the Peanut Butter & Co. brand, carried at most major and gourmet supermarkets)
- Reduced-fat low-sodium chicken broth
- Reduced-fat low-sodium beef broth
- Canned tomatoes—crushed and whole
- Canned chickpeas
- Canned beets

- Canned navy beans
- Canned kidney beans
- Solid pack pumpkin (not pumpkin-pie mix)
- Crushed pineapple (packed in juice)
- High-quality bottled pasta sauce
- Unsweetened coconut
- Breadcrumbs: panko, Italian-style whole wheat, or regular
- Balsamic vinegar
- Reduced-sodium soy sauce

- Low-sodium Worcestershire sauce
- Pure maple syrup
- Honey
- Ketchup
- Onions
- Garlic

THE PUREES: HOW-TO

Step 1

Set aside time every week.

Plan to go grocery shopping once a week to buy all the fruits and vegetables you need for the week's worth of purees. In addition, plan to spend one hour a week making the purees. I have a standing date with my husband in the kitchen every Sunday night after the kids have gone to bed. We do a good catch-up and planning meeting for the week ahead while I puree the night away (really, it only takes an hour to make a ton of purees). And when I'm done, I feel so virtuous.

Which vegetables do you buy? Decide which you think your child is most likely to eat. If he is very picky about green vegetables, I'd suggest starting with cauliflower, butternut squash, zucchini, and yellow squash, because they're easier to conceal.

And how much? Start with one pound of each vegetable, or one head of cauliflower, or one butternut squash. Once you get a stash of purees in your freezer, you can simply replenish it as necessary each week.

You can steal a few minutes here and there at other times during the week, too: when I've got the oven on for baking, for example, I'll throw in a couple of sweet potatoes to roast alongside whatever else I'm cooking.

Step 2

Prepare vegetables and fruits.

1 Wash the veggies and fruits and drain in a colander.

2 Lay out a sheet of waxed paper, a dish towel, or a recycled paper shopping bag (cut so that you can open it out) to collect the trimmings.

3 Prepare the vegetables and fruit as shown on the chart beginning on page 28.

• Sometimes, instead of using fresh produce, I'll use frozen veggies or just open a can. Canned beets and pineapple, for instance, make fine purees (buy pineapple that's packed in natural juices, not sugar syrup). Drain before pureeing.

- If I'm really in a hurry, I'll sometimes use the cut-up fresh vegetables that are sold in supermarkets. Check that they look fresh, not dried or discolored.

4 Remember that the good thing about fruits is that they don't need to be cooked. In certain recipes, even the vegetables don't need to be cooked—just finely chopped in the food processor. You'll see that I've noted this in recipe headnotes, wherever possible.

Step 3

Cook the vegetables.

Steaming is a great way to cook vegetables because it preserves their nutrients. You can use a rice steamer, a collapsible steamer basket, or a pasta pot with drainer.

1 Peel, trim, and cut up the vegetable as shown on the chart on page 28.

2 Put about 1 inch of water in the bottom of a pot. Add a steamer basket (without the vegetables), cover, and bring the water to a boil. (Or follow the instructions that come with your rice steamer.)
- If you don't have any other type of steamer, you can also steam in a saucepan: bring ½ inch water to a boil,

add the veggies, cover, and steam. But be careful—the water evaporates quickly; if it does, the vegetables may burn.

3 Place the vegetables in the steamer—up to a double layer will steam well—cover, and steam the number of minutes recommended on page 28.
- If you're steaming several different batches of vegetables, start each batch with fresh water. Particularly with green vegetables, the steaming water gets bitter and it will turn the vegetables bitter, too.

4 Drain the vegetables in a colander.

Roasting is our friend. It is an easy way to cook sweet potatoes, beets, and butternut squash—just throw the vegetable unpeeled in the oven, set a timer, and forget about it while you go check your e-mail or make a fort with your kids.

1 Preheat the oven to 400°F.

2 Prepare the vegetables as recommended

on page 28, place them on a foil-lined baking sheet, and roast until tender.

3 Set aside until cool enough to handle. Then peel beets, or scoop sweet potato or squash out of the peel with a table-spoon—it should glide right out.

Microwave cooking is fast and requires no special cooking equipment. Since all microwave ovens are different, it's impossi-ble to give hard and fast cooking times, but you'll get a handle on it quickly with a lit-tle trial and error.

1 Peel, trim, and cut up the vegetables.

2 Put the vegetables in a glass or ceramic container (no metal!). Add 2 tablespoons of water. Loosely cover with microwave-able plastic wrap, a microwave-safe lid, or waxed paper.

3 Microwave in 1-minute increments until the vegetables are tender when pierced with the tip of a sharp knife.

Step 4

Puree.

1 Put the veggies and fruits into a food processor or blender, secure the lid, press the "on" button ("grind" on a mini-food processor), and puree until smooth and creamy. Generally, this takes about two minutes.

• Mash bananas and avocados with a fork before pureeing.

• Puree large quantities in a stan-dard-sized food processor; a mini-chop-per works best for small quantities.

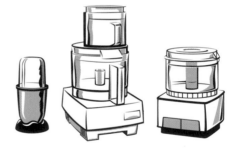

2 You may need to add a teaspoon or so of water to cauliflower, carrots, and broc-coli to make a smooth, creamy puree.

3 Let warm purees cool.

Step 5

Portion and package the purees.

1 Measure the purees into ½-cup portions (sometimes I make ¼-cup portions, depending on the recipe) and package in small zipper-lock plastic bags if you plan to use the puree within a few days (or in freezer bags for longer storage).

2 Using a permanent marker, label each bag with the type and amount of puree and the date. For example: ½ cup spinach, 9/24/07.

3 Refrigerate purees that will be used in the next couple of days; freeze the rest.
• I use plastic storage bins in both the fridge and the freezer to hold the bagged purees. The bags stay more organized, and it's easier to keep track of which ones to use first.

Step 6

Cook!

Now that you have your kitchen and pantry stocked, you're ready to use the recipes that start on page 43.

1 Choose the purees you need for the recipes you are cooking.

2 Scan the recipes and choose the purees you need. Always use older purees (check the date) first.

3 Thaw bags of frozen puree in the microwave (the time will depend on your microwave), or soak in a bowl of hot water until soft

4 Snip the corner of the bag with scissors to squeeze out the puree.

5 Use the purees just like any other ingredients—in my recipes or stirred into prepared food for an instant nutrition boost. (For example, you can fortify a jar of store-bought pasta sauce with almost any of the purees—add the puree gradually, tasting and checking the color as you go. You know what your kids will eat.)

VEGETABLE PUREES: HOW-TO

Avocados

Prep: Cut in half lengthwise, whack the blade of a chef's knife into the seed, twist to loosen, and remove. Scoop the flesh out of the peel.

Puree: Mash well in a bowl with a fork until very smooth, then puree in a food processor or blender for about 2 minutes. When storing, squeeze air out of bag before sealing.

Beets

Prep: Leave them whole (trim any stems to 1 inch) and unpeeled.

Cook: Wrap in aluminum foil and roast at 400°F for about 1 hour (they're done when they can be pierced with tip of a sharp knife).

Puree: After peeling, place in a food processor or blender for about 2 minutes.

Broccoli

Prep: Cut into florets.

Cook: Steam for 6 to 7 minutes. Florets should be tender but still bright green (if they turn an olive green color, they're overcooked).

Puree: In a food processor or blender for about 2 minutes. Add a few teaspoons of water if needed for a smooth, creamy texture.

Butternut Squash

Prep: Cut off the stem, cut squash in half lengthwise and scrape out seeds.

Cook: Roast the halves on a cookie sheet, flesh-side down, at 400°F for 45 to 50 minutes.

Puree: Scoop out the flesh and puree in a food processor or blender for about 2 minutes.

Carrots

Prep: Peel, trim the ends, and cut into 3-inch chunks.

Cook: Steam for 10 to 12 minutes.

Puree: In a food processor or blender for about 2 minutes, with a few teaspoons of water if needed for a smooth texture.

Cauliflower

Prep: Cut off florets and discard core.

Cook: Steam for 8 to 10 minutes.

Puree: In a food processor or blender for about 2 minutes, with a few teaspoons of water if needed for a smooth, creamy texture.

Peas

Prep: None at all for frozen peas!

Cook: Steam frozen peas for about 2 minutes; if thawed, reduce steaming time to 30 to 60 seconds.

Puree: In a food processor or blender for about 2 minutes, until very smooth and creamy. Add water if necessary.

Red Bell Peppers

Prep: Cut in half through the stem end. Remove the stem, seeds, and white membrane.

Cook: Steam for 10 to 12 minutes.

Puree: In a food processor or blender for about 2 minutes, until smooth.

Spinach

Prep: No prep *at all* for baby spinach. For mature spinach, fold leaves in half lengthwise with the stem outside, then strip the stem off the leaf.

Cook: Steam for 30 to 40 seconds, or cook in a skillet with 1 tablespoon water for about 90 seconds, or just until wilted.

Puree: In a food processor or blender for about 2 minutes, until smooth and creamy.

Sweet Potatoes

Prep: Do not peel. Cut into quarters, if steaming. Leave whole, if roasting.

Cook: Steam for 40 to 45 minutes. Roast at 400°F for 50 to 60 minutes.

Puree: Scoop out the flesh and puree in a food processor or blender.

Zucchini and Summer Squash

Prep: Trim off the ends and cut into 1-inch pieces.

Cook: Steam for 6 to 8 minutes.

Puree: In a food processor or blender for about 2 minutes, until smooth

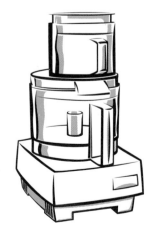

FRUIT PUREES: HOW-TO

Apples

Prep: May be peeled or not. Quarter and core.

Puree: In a food processor or blender for about 2 minutes.

Bananas

Prep: Use ripe bananas for the smoothest, sweetest puree. Peel.

Puree: Mash with a fork on a cutting board (bananas jump around in a bowl) then puree in a food processor or blender for about 2 minutes.

Blueberries, Raspberries, and Strawberries

Prep: Thaw, if frozen. Cut or pull off the stems for strawberries

Puree: In a food processor or blender for about 2 minutes.

Cantaloupe

Prep: Cut the melon in half, then scoop out the seeds. Cut the melon into wedges and pare off the rind.

Puree: In a food processor or blender for about 2 minutes.

Cherries

Prep: If fresh, stem the cherries and pit them with a cherry pitter. If frozen, thaw them.

Puree: In a food processor or blender for about 2 minutes.

Pineapple

Prep: Cut off the stem. Pare off the rind, cutting deeply enough to remove the prickly "eyes." Quarter it lengthwise, cut out the core, and cut into chunks.

Puree: In a food processor or blender for about 2 minutes.

The Basics: Cooking Rice, Pasta, Chicken, and Beef

Some of the recipes in this book call for a basic knowledge of how to cook rice and pasta. For those who need it, here's a refresher course.

Cooking rice

I use brown rice, which still has the nutrient-rich bran and hull intact. If you're using white rice, cut the water to 1⅓ cups, and the cooking time to 15 to 18 minutes. You can mix the white and brown rice to ease your family into eating brown rice.

Stovetop method:
1 Place 1 cup brown rice, 1¾ cups water, and a pinch of salt in a saucepan.
2 Bring to a boil, cover, reduce the heat to very low, and simmer until the rice is tender and all of the water has been absorbed, 30 to 40 minutes.
3 Turn off the heat and let stand, covered, 5 minutes.

Electric rice cooker method:
There are several brands of cookers on the market. Follow the instructions that come with your cooker.

Cooking pasta

Whole-wheat pasta may be too "brown" for some children. Mix it with multi-grain or semolina pasta, and gradually move toward whole-wheat only.

1 Bring a large pot of salted water to a boil over high heat.
2 Add the pasta and cook according to the package directions until al dente.
3 Drain pasta carefully (watch out for splashing water) in a colander.

Pureeing chicken and beef

You can sneak chicken or beef into your kids' food by cooking and pureeing it first.

1 Sprinkle skinless boneless chicken breast or cutlets, or beef steak, with salt and pepper.
2 Coat a large nonstick skillet with cooking spray and heat over medium-high heat. When the skillet is hot, add 1 tablespoon olive oil, and then the meat. For chicken cutlets, cook 4 to 5 minutes per; for chicken breast and beef steak, cook 5 minutes per side, reduce heat to low, cover, and cook 9 to 10 minutes longer.
3 Let cool slightly before cutting into pieces.
4 Transfer to the food processor and process until finely ground. You can slowly add drops of water for a creamy texture.

WHAT EVERY PARENT SHOULD KNOW ABOUT NUTRITION

Joy Bauer is our nutrition guru. I met her a couple of years ago when I went to her for help in dropping a few hard-to-lose post-pregnancy pounds. She convinced me that healthy food could be both delicious and easy to prepare. Joy is also a hard-working mother of three, and she really gets how important it is to be able to shop and cook efficiently. She has weighed in on all of our recipes and given her stamp of approval as well as important nutritional advice.

"**Y**OU CAN'T control every bite your child eats, and you wouldn't want to—it's important for kids to develop control and confidence when it comes to what they eat. But we all know that proper nutrition increases energy, prevents injury and enhances healing, improves academic performance, and even has a positive effect on moods (if you've ever picked your child up from a party where he's polished off birthday cake, ice cream, and a goody bag full of treats, you've probably experienced the ups and downs of what I call 'blood sugar chaos' in the hours that follow).

So what should we be feeding our kids? There are lots of different nutritional fads and theories making the rounds these days (and just what is a 'serving,' anyway?). It's all gotten to be more than a little confusing. And the feedback I get from parents is that they don't have the time to sort it all out.

As a nutritionist and a mother, I'm trying to juggle it all, too. It's just not practical to be counting and measuring foods all the time to be sure that your kids are getting what they need.

And you don't have to.

The beauty of the recipes in this book is that we've already thought about the nutrition. But it's a good idea for parents to have some general sense of nutrition, so I'm going to give you the basic nutritional guidelines (set out in the chart on the following pages) that I use in my own home.

It's simple: instead of quantities or servings, I think in terms of general categories of foods that my kids need to be eating every day—vegetables, fruits, protein, whole grains, and calcium-rich foods including milk. And then I choose the foods from each category that offer the most nutritional 'bang for the bite.'

The most important thing you can do is offer *variety*. That way, your kids are sure to get a variety of nutrients, and you don't have to spend time worrying about milligrams of vitamin this or that.

There are measures of what constitutes a 'serving,' and you'll see that information in the guidelines that follow. But you don't have to go so far as to measure every portion. It really is enough just to offer the foods regularly. You can't control how much they eat anyway, right?

And while it's great that the recipes in this book, with their 'sneak it in' technique, remove the stress of getting kids to eat vegetables through a little harmless deception, I agree with Jessica that you should by no means stop putting at least one visible veggie on the table at lunch and dinner. For example, serve steamed green beans or sautéed broccoli, or go raw with crunchy baby carrots, sugar snap peas, or red, yellow, or orange bell pepper strips—serve them plain, or with some of the delicious dips on pages 123 and 127. You want your kids to get used to seeing vegetables and, of course, eating them. Which ones you choose and how you cook them—steamed, roasted, microwaved, or stir-fried in olive oil—that's up to you. Trust me, even if your kids don't go for the veggies immediately, they will eventually."

EASY NUTRITIONAL GUIDELINES FOR CHILDREN

Vegetables

 3+ A DAY!

Some of the vegetables with the highest nutrient content are broccoli, bell peppers (all colors), spinach, tomatoes, carrots, squash, and Brussels sprouts. Try to get at least **three** of these into your child every day—1½ to 2½ cups total, either in purees or as vegetable side dishes. In my experience, the five top vegetables for nutrition *and* kid friendliness are, in this order:

- **red bell peppers**
- **baby carrots**
- **broccoli**
- **tomatoes**
- **sugar snap peas**

As popular with kids but a bit less nutritious are: **green beans, peas, corn, cucumbers,** and **lettuce.** Frozen peas and corn, especially, can be prepared in a matter of minutes.

One serving = 1 cup raw, or ½ cup cooked

Fresh Fruits

 2 A DAY!

Some of the best fruits are strawberries, raspberries, blackberries, blueberries, oranges, red apples, bananas, pink grapefruit, melon, kiwi fruit, and red grapes. Shoot for at least **two** a day. And remember, the actual fruit is more nutritious than its juice.

One serving = 1 item, such as an orange or apple, or ¾ cup berries, or ¾ cup fruit salad

Whole Grains

 3 A DAY!

Whole grains are grains that contain all three parts of the natural grain: bran, endosperm, and germ (all three elements make whole grains highly nutritious). That means brown or wild rice instead of white, whole-grain or whole-wheat bread instead of white, and whole-grain or whole-wheat pasta instead of regular, white (refined) semolina.

When reading bread and cereal labels, don't be fooled by terms like "multi-grain" or "5-grain"—the first ingredient should contain the word "whole" or "oats." Aim for at least **three** servings a day and don't hesitate to mix white rice with brown or wild, and regular pasta with whole wheat if your kids balk.

One serving = ½ cup cooked rice, pasta, or whole-grain couscous; 1 slice whole-grain bread; ½ cup dry oatmeal or 1 cup whole-grain ready-to-eat breakfast cereal (ideally with 6 or fewer grams of sugar, and 3 or more grams of fiber per serving)

Calcium-Rich Foods

 A DAY!

The number-one source of calcium for children (after the age of two) is skim or lowfat (1%) milk. But don't forget other lowfat dairy products such as lowfat yogurt and cottage cheese and reduced-fat cheese—aim for **three plus** servings a day. (Lowfat dairy can be a better source of calcium than full fat, by volume, because removing the artery-clogging fat often makes room for more calcium.) Other good nondairy sources are:

- **Green vegetables** (particularly broccoli and kale)
- **Beans** (specifically white beans and soy beans)
- **Tofu** (best if the label says "good source of calcium")
- **Calcium-fortified foods** such as some brands of whole-grain waffles and orange juice. Calcium needs go up as children age. Children ages 9 through 18 need 1,300 mg of calcium, or approximately 4 servings a day of calcium-rich food.

One serving = 1 cup milk, yogurt, or calcium-fortified juice, ½ to 1 cup beans (especially white beans and soybeans) or broccoli, or 4 ounces of calcium-rich tofu

Lean Source of Protein

The best sources of protein for children are: turkey breast, chicken breast, pork tenderloin, fish and seafood, tofu, turkey/veggie burgers, lowfat dairy, edamame (fresh soybeans), beans—such as black, kidney, navy, and pinto—and eggs.

Here are some examples of protein amounts, in grams, for several foods that your kids are likely to be eating:

- **Grilled chicken (3 ounces or 1 palm-sized piece):** *21 grams*
- **Turkey burger (4 ounces):** *21 grams*
- **Yogurt (6-ounce container):** *6–8 grams*
- **Lowfat (1%) milk (1 cup):** *8 grams*
- **Peanut butter (2 tablespoons):** *8 grams*
- **Tofu (3 ounces):** *7 grams*
- **1 egg:** *6 grams*
- **Nuts (¼ cup):** *6–8 grams*
- **Veggie burger:** *5–10 grams*
- **1 slice pizza:** *12 grams*
- **1 string cheese:** *8 grams*

A rule of thumb is that kids need to eat approximately half their body weight in grams of protein a day. For example, a 70 pound child needs about 35 grams of protein a day.

Fats

You also want to minimize **saturated and trans fats** in your child's diet. I use only low- or nonfat dairy in my home and keep a trans-fat-free kitchen. That means no commercially prepared baked goods or fried foods containing hydrogenated vegetable oil. The payoff is that you won't have to sweat the occasional cookie or doughnut from the local bakery when the kids are out and about. The fats you do want to encourage are:

- **Monounsaturated fats,** found in olive and canola oil, nuts, and avocados.
- **Omega-3 fats,** found in fatty fish (such as wild salmon and sardines), walnuts, flax-seed, and omega-3-fortified eggs.

Fiber

We're all hearing a lot about **fiber** these days. Insoluble fiber helps keep the pipes clean! That is, it helps prevent and treat constipation, and helps to keep the digestive system running smoothly. It has also been shown to protect against obesity, heart disease, and type 2 diabetes. Another kind of fiber, soluble fiber, helps whisk cholesterol away before it's digested, and can stabilize blood-sugar levels in kids. If you offer a variety of vegetables, fruits, and whole grains, your children should be getting plenty of fiber.

WHAT'S IN THAT VEGGIE?

1/4 Avocado
(55 calories)

- Avocados are the only vegetables that are loaded with monounsaturated fat, which helps lower cholesterol levels in the blood to keep kids heart-healthy.
- They're also a super source of soluble fiber, which helps stabilize blood-sugar levels.
- And they're full of vitamin E, which protects healthy cells and helps heal kids' cuts and scrapes.

1 Cup Beets
(58 calories)

- Beets are chock full of two different antioxidants that help protect healthy cells against damage all over the body.
- The folic acid in beets also help keep kids' cells growing and functioning the way they should.
- And beets are good for heart health and for keeping kids' blood pressure regulated, because they provide a nice amount of potassium.

1 Cup Broccoli
(30 calories)

- Along with all other veggies in the cruciferous family, broccoli is important because it contains natural substances that may help the body fight certain cancers.
- Broccoli also helps heal kids' cuts and wounds—it's a particularly good source of vitamin C.
- And, for a vegetable, broccoli can't be beat in helping build strong bones and teeth (it's a great nondairy source of calcium—better absorbed by the body than spinach).

1 Cup Butternut Squash
(63 calories)

- The deep orange color of this winter squash reminds us that it contains beta carotene, which is great for keeping your child's eyes and skin healthy.
- Plus, this vegetable contains potassium, which is important for heart health.

 1 Cup Carrots
(52 calories)

- Carrots are terrific for your child's skin and eyes because they're loaded with beta carotene.
- And they're great for keeping the pipes clean because they contain a good amount of insoluble fiber.

 1 Cup Cauliflower
(25 calories)

- Cauliflower is another member of the important cruciferous family of veggies that may help our bodies fight off certain types of cancers.
- Cauliflower may help kids resist infections (it's a good source of vitamin C).

 1 Cup Pumpkin
(30 calories)

- Pumpkin helps build healthy hearts because it's high in potassium.
- Its pretty orange color also signals that pumpkin is a rich source of beta carotene, which helps keep kids' skin bright and eyesight sharp, and encourages overall good health.

 1 Cup Peas
(134 calories)

- Peas are a good source of folate, so it's good for your child's overall heart health.
- Peas are also great source of fiber (both soluble and insoluble), which helps stabilize kids blood sugars and keep their digestion running smoothly.

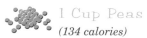 1 Cup Red Pepper
(39 calories)

- Red peppers are the single best way to get vitamin C into your children, which may help them to fight off infections and heal cuts and scrapes.
- And thanks to their beautiful, rich red color, they're high in several antioxidants that help protect healthy cells throughout the body.

1 Cup Cooked Spinach
(40 calories)

- Spinach is your best bet for folic acid, which helps keep cells all over the body growing and functioning well.
- And it's an incredible non-animal-protein source of iron, which delivers oxygen all over the body, providing much-needed energy to kids' muscles.
- Spinach also helps regulate blood sugar and keeps your children's hearts healthy because it's high in potassium and magnesium.

 1 Cup Summer Squash and Zucchini
(20 calories)

- Summer squash and zucchini helps keep children's skin glowing because it provides vitamin C.
- The antioxidant called lutein in summer squash helps keep kids bright-eyed.

 1 Small Sweet Potato
(112 calories)

- Sweet potatoes help stabilize kids' blood sugar levels by providing soluble fiber.
- And they're good for skin, eyes, and all-over good health because they're rich in beta carotene and other antioxidants.

 *Joy: The thing that destroys the good stuff in veggies is cooking them in too much water. The water-soluble vitamins (particularly vitamin C) leak out into the water and you lose them. Steaming, microwaving, and roasting are better than boiling. Overcooking can also diminish nutritional value, so cook vegetables just until tender, and no longer.*

WHAT'S IN THAT FRUIT?

 1 Apple
(80 calories)

- Apples help prevent damage to healthy cells because they're high in antioxidants—particularly the skin of Red Delicious apples, so don't peel them!
- And they're high in soluble fiber, which helps regulate blood-sugar levels.

 1 Banana
(105 calories)

- Bananas help regulate kids' blood pressure and keep their hearts healthy (bananas contain more potassium than most fruits and as much as many vegetables).
- They also help children's bodies produce important hormones and enzymes, and help keep young brains fit, because they're a good source of vitamin B6.

 1 Cup Blueberries
(84 calories)

- Blueberries are one of the best possible fruits when it comes to protecting healthy cells. Studies have shown that they contain a high amount of antioxidants, (shown to lower cholesterol, sharpen memory, and fight certain cancers).
- And they're great for keeping the system moving! (Blueberries have a nice amount of insoluble fiber.)

 1 Cup Cantaloupe
(54 calories)

- Cantaloupe is super for kids' eyesight and eye health—its orange color shows that it contains beta carotene.
- And it's terrific at helping kids heal cuts and scrapes, because it provides young bodies with vitamin C.

 1 Cup Cherries
(78 calories)

- When your kids eat cherries, they're getting antioxidants called anthocyanins, which help grow healthy brains and may help fight certain cancers as well.

1 Cup Pineapple
(74 calories)

- Pineapple helps kids' digestion, while it works to reduce inflammation and swelling.
- It's also outstanding at helping kids heal when they fall and scrape their knees, because it's packed full of vitamin C.

 1 Cup Raspberries
(64 calories)

- Raspberries are the most kid-friendly source of insoluble fiber—they're loaded with it!
- And they're a good source of antioxidants called anthocyanins, which help to keep kids' brains fit and help our bodies fight certain cancers.

 1 Cup Strawberries
(53 calories)

- Strawberries are super at helping kids heal cuts and scrapes, and keeping their skin glowing—they're the very best berry source for vitamin C.
- And, like other berries and cherries, strawberries are high in anthocyanins, which are good for brain health and for fighting some cancers.

Joy: The important nutrients in vegetables and fruits are vitamins, minerals, fiber and phytonutrients (naturally occurring plant compounds that help fight disease and enhance overall health, such as lycopene, anthocyanin, and lutein). Deeply colored vegetables and fruits, such as beets, carrots, and berries, are typically the most nutritious, so load up!

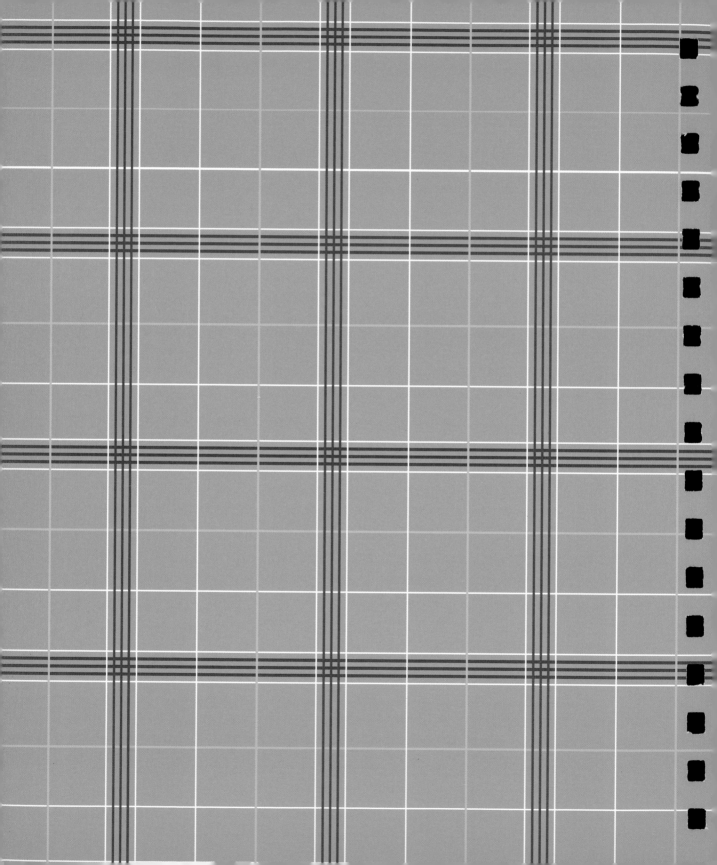

THE
RECIPES

THE DECEPTION BEGINS

YOU'RE READY to go. Your kitchen and pantry are stocked, and you've tucked away a nice assortment of purees in your fridge or freezer.

Most of the dishes use one or two purees. At the top of the recipes you will see a collection of illustrations of fruits and vegetables that represent all of the purees you will need, plus options. This will help you choose which recipe you want to make on the basis of which fruits and vegetables you think you can sneak by your child, as well as which purees you have on hand.

If your child is picky about green vegetables, start with a recipe that uses a white, yellow, or orange vegetable, such as cauliflower, butternut squash, yellow squash, zucchini, sweet potato, or carrots. These purees blend easily into a variety of both homemade and store-bought foods. As you get more comfortable making the purees, you can push the envelope and move onto the greater challenge—green vegetables. That will happen soon, I promise!

People ask me if they can substitute purees in the recipes. The answer is, again, it depends on your child. I developed the recipes so that the vegetables would be as invisible as possible, and even your super picky eaters wouldn't notice. Some children freak out when they see any green at all. Others can handle it. You know best what you're dealing with.

I've given substitutes where possible. (If you're in a bind, most of the recipes work without the purees.) If you're preparing a dish that uses two different purees, you can always double up on one (if your recipe calls for ½ cup spinach puree and ½ cup carrot, you can use one cup of either, instead).

You can always substitute one green puree for another, except in the dessert recipes. Some vegetable purees just taste funny in sweets. Some also make baked goods a little gummy. So for desserts, I recommend sticking to exactly what's called for in the recipes.

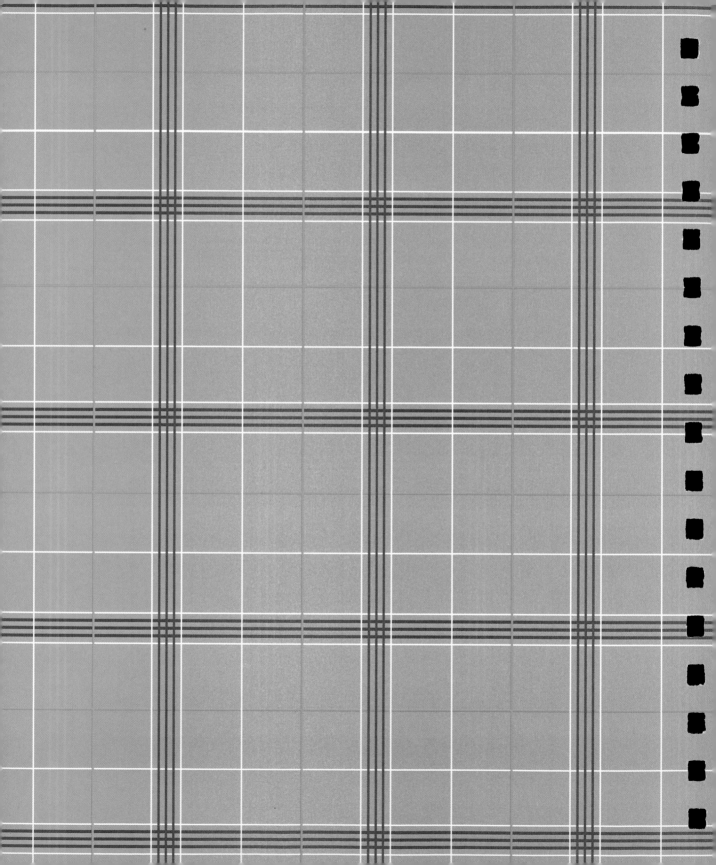

BREAKFAST

French Toast **49**

Applesauce Muffins **50**

Scrambled Eggs **53**

Banana Bread **54**

Pancakes **57**

Peanut Butter and Banana Muffins . . . **58**

Coffee Cake **61**

Green Eggs **62**

Peanut Butter and Jelly Muffins **63**

Blueberry Lemon Muffins **65**

Baked Egg Puffs **67**

Oatmeal **68**

French Toast

(WITH BANANA OR PINEAPPLE OR SWEET POTATO OR PUMPKIN OR CARROT OR BUTTERNUT SQUASH)

Some children are suspicious of the "specks" in whole-grain bread, and a dusting of sugar serves nicely as camouflage! A shaker for confectioners' sugar is one of the best investments I've ever made.

Prep: 3 minutes • Total: 10 minutes • Serves 4

- **4 large eggs**
- **2 tablespoons banana or pineapple or sweet potato or carrot or butternut squash puree, or canned pumpkin**
- **¼ teaspoon cinnamon**
- **4 slices whole-wheat bread**
- **Nonstick cooking spray**
- **2 teaspoons trans-fat-free soft tub margarine spread**
- **Pure maple syrup, confectioners' sugar, or fresh fruit, for serving**
- **Flaxseed meal (optional)**

1 In a shallow bowl, whisk the eggs, puree, and cinnamon. Add the bread slices and turn them in the mixture to soak for 30 seconds to 1 minute (any longer and the bread will get soggy).

2 Coat a nonstick griddle or large nonstick skillet with cooking spray and set it over medium-high heat. When the pan is hot, add the margarine. When the margarine sizzles, add the soaked bread slices (sprinkle with flaxseed if you like) and cook until golden brown on the outside, 2 to 3 minutes per side. Serve warm with syrup, confectioners' sugar, or fruit.

Sascha: *Even when I'm late for school in the morning, my mom still makes this for breakfast. It's really fast.*

Applesauce Muffins

(WITH BUTTERNUT SQUASH OR CARROT)

A crunchy streusel topping makes these muffins irresistible!

Prep: 20 minutes • Total: 40 minutes • Makes 12 muffins

- **Nonstick cooking spray**

TOPPING
- **⅔ cup old-fashioned oats**
- **¼ cup firmly packed light or dark brown sugar**
- **1 teaspoon cinnamon**
- **2 tablespoons trans-fat-free soft tub margarine spread, melted**

BATTER
- **1 ½ cups all-purpose flour**
- **1 cup old-fashioned oats**
- **1 teaspoon baking powder**
- **½ teaspoon baking soda**
- **½ teaspoon cinnamon**
- **1 cup unsweetened applesauce**
- **½ cup nonfat (skim) milk**
- **½ cup butternut squash or carrot puree**
- **½ cup firmly packed light or dark brown sugar**
- **¼ cup vegetable or canola oil**
- **1 large egg**

1 Preheat the oven to 400°F. Coat a 12-cup muffin tin with cooking spray or line with paper baking cups.

2 To make the topping, stir together the oats, sugar, and cinnamon in a bowl. Stir in the margarine.

3 To make the batter, combine the flour, oats, baking powder, baking soda, and cinnamon in a large mixing bowl or zipper-lock bag and stir or shake to mix. In a second bowl, mix the applesauce with the milk, vegetable puree, sugar, oil, and egg with a wooden spoon. Add the flour mixture slowly, stirring until just moistened. Do not overmix—the batter is supposed to be lumpy.

4 Divide the batter evenly among the muffin cups and sprinkle with the streusel topping. Bake until the topping is lightly browned and a toothpick comes out clean when inserted into the center of the muffins, 18 to 20 minutes. Turn the muffins out onto a rack and serve warm or cool.

Saying No, Artfully

S AYING "NO" teaches children that the world is full of necessary limits, and builds a trusting relationship between you and your child. When my kids complain to me that their friends get to eat what I consider "junk," I try to answer honestly yet firmly and sympathetically. For example: "I see that you're disappointed about the cereal in our house, but eating cereal that is made of a lot of sugar is not good for your teeth or body."

Along the way, I've come up with a few guidelines (although of course each family has its own set of rules):

1 I try not to be ambivalent or apologetic about my rules.

2 I always explain my reasons.

3 I point out that all families eat differently, and that every household has different rules. Some make kids happy, some mad; but rules are made to keep kids safe and healthy.

4 I empathize with their feelings, but I don't give in. I find that this re- assures them, and it confirms my credibility and consistency.

Scrambled Eggs

(*WITH CAULIFLOWER*)

The cauliflower puree simply "melts" into the fluffy eggs.

Prep: 3 minutes • Total: 6 minutes • Serves 2

- 2 large eggs
- 4 large egg whites
- ¼ cup reduced-fat sour cream
- ½ cup cauliflower puree
- 2 tablespoons grated Parmesan
- Pinch of salt
- Nonstick cooking spray
- 1 teaspoon olive oil

1 In a large bowl, whisk together the eggs, egg whites, sour cream, cauliflower puree, Parmesan, and salt.

2 Coat a large nonstick skillet with cooking spray, then set the pan over medium-high heat. When the pan is hot, add the oil. Add the egg mixture, reduce the heat to low, and cook, stirring frequently with a silicone spatula, until the eggs are scrambled—firm but nice and moist—2 to 3 minutes.

Joy: *Hidden cauliflower puree provides kids with half of the daily value for vitamin C. With more than 19 grams of protein per serving, these scrambled eggs pack a powerful protein punch!*

Banana Bread

(WITH CAULIFLOWER)

This treat works all day long—my kids like it for breakfast, lunch, snacks, or dessert. If you're out of cauliflower puree, add one more banana. For an extra-special treat, sprinkle batter with the streusel topping on page 50.

Prep: 10 minutes • Total: 70 minutes • Makes a 9x5-inch loaf, or 2 mini loaves

- Nonstick cooking spray
- ³⁄₄ cup whole-wheat flour
- ¹⁄₂ cup all-purpose flour
- ¹⁄₂ teaspoon baking soda
- ¹⁄₄ teaspoon baking powder
- ¹⁄₂ teaspoon salt
- ¹⁄₂ teaspoon cinnamon (optional)
- ¹⁄₂ cup firmly packed light or dark brown sugar
- ¹⁄₄ cup canola or vegetable oil
- 2 large egg whites
- 1¹⁄₂ cups banana puree
- ¹⁄₂ cup cauliflower puree
- 1 teaspoon pure vanilla extract

1 Preheat the oven to 350°F. Coat a 9x5-inch loaf pan, or 2 mini pans, with cooking spray.

2 In a bowl or a zipper-lock bag, mix the flours with the baking soda, baking powder, salt, and cinnamon, if using. Set aside.

3 In a large mixing bowl, mix the sugar and oil with a wooden spoon until well combined. Mix in the egg whites, banana and cauliflower purees, and vanilla. Add the flour mixture and mix just until combined.

4 Pour the batter into the loaf pan. Bake until a toothpick inserted into the center comes out clean, 55 to 60 minutes for the large loaf, 25 to 30 minutes for the mini loaves. Let cool on a rack for 5 minutes, then turn the bread out of the pan to cool before serving.

Julian: *I spread peanut butter on this. Yum.*

Pancakes

(WITH SWEET POTATO)

Sweet potato puree both sweetens and boosts the nutrition of this simple, quick breakfast.

Prep: 3 minutes • Total: 6–10 minutes • Serves 4

- **1 cup water**
- ½ cup sweet potato puree
- **¼ teaspoon cinnamon or pumpkin pie spice (optional)**
- **1 cup pancake mix**
- **Nonstick cooking spray**
- **1 tablespoon canola or vegetable oil**
- **Pure maple syrup, for serving**

1 In a large bowl, mix the water, sweet potato puree, and cinnamon or pumpkin pie spice, if using. Add the pancake mix and stir just to combine—the batter should be lumpy.

2 Coat a griddle or large nonstick skillet with cooking spray and set it over medium-high heat. When the pan is hot, add the oil, and spoon the batter onto the griddle or pan, using ¼ cup batter for each pancake.

3 Cook until bubbles form on top of the pancakes and the batter is set, 2 to 3 minutes. Then use a spatula to flip the pancakes and cook them until golden brown on the other side, 2 to 3 minutes.

Sascha: My mom makes pancake batter at night and puts it in the fridge so it's ready for my breakfast in the morning.

Peanut Butter and Banana Muffins

(WITH CARROT OR CAULIFLOWER AND BANANA)

I discovered that adding half the brown sugar at the end of mixing creates a spectacular, crunchy exterior on top of these muffins.

Prep: 10 minutes • Total: 35 minutes • Makes 12 muffins • Packable

- **Nonstick cooking spray**
- **1 cup firmly packed light or dark brown sugar**
- **½ cup natural peanut butter**
- **½ cup carrot or cauliflower puree**
- **½ cup banana puree**
- **1 large egg white**
- **1 cup whole-wheat flour**
- **1 teaspoon baking powder**
- **1 teaspoon baking soda**
- **½ teaspoon salt**

1 Preheat the oven to 350°F. Coat a 12-cup muffin tin with cooking spray or line with paper baking cups.

2 In a large mixing bowl, mix ½ cup of the brown sugar with the peanut butter, the vegetable and banana purees, and the egg white, using a wooden spoon.

3 Put the flour, baking powder, baking soda, and salt in a bowl or zipper-lock bag and stir or shake to mix. Add to the bowl with the peanut butter mixture and stir just to combine (the batter will be a little lumpy—do not overmix). Add the remaining ½ cup of brown sugar and stir once or twice.

4 Divide the batter among the muffin cups and bake until the muffins are lightly browned and a toothpick comes out clean when inserted into the center, 15 to 20 minutes. Turn the muffins out onto a rack to cool.

5 Store in an airtight container at room temperature for up to 2 days, or wrap individually and freeze for up to 1 month.

(OTHER) MOTHERS KNOW BEST
(PART 1)

"James says he'll take a lick but not a bite until he knows he likes what he's about to eat. Second, he says it helps if he can have a toy at the table while he's trying something new. And third, if he hears an adult say that they love it, he'll try it. I've also found that if he is at the house of someone familiar, like a friend, and the friend is having something he might have resisted at home—like milk with dinner—then he will learn to like it, because he wants to be like his friend."

— Sarah, New York City
MOTHER OF JAMES, 4

"This is how I get Charlie to eat a healthy dessert of yogurt: I let her sprinkle a tiny amount of sprinkles into it. She loves it. In fact, it's probably her most requested dessert."

—Kate, Los Angeles
MOTHER OF CHARLIE, 3

"My girls eat broccoli with melted cheese and cream cheese in celery stalks. Fruit skewers are a big hit—long kebabs with strawberries, grapes, raspberries, and pineapple chunks, which they dip in strawberry yogurt. They also love roasted potatoes (in olive oil) and homemade French fries (with ketchup)."

—Alexandra, Washington, D.C.
MOTHER OF ELLIOT, 5, AND HARPER, 2

Coffee Cake
(WITH BUTTERNUT SQUASH)

This is a favorite at our house. I make it when we have company on the weekends.

Prep: 15 minutes • Total: 75 minutes • Serves 10

BATTER
- **Nonstick cooking spray**
- **1 cup firmly packed light or dark brown sugar**
- **4 tablespoons trans-fat-free soft tub margarine spread**
- **1¼ cups lowfat (1%) buttermilk or nonfat (skim) milk**
- **1 cup reduced-fat sour cream**
- **1 large egg**
- **2 teaspoons pure vanilla extract**
- **2 cups whole-wheat flour**
- **2 teaspoons baking powder**
- **½ teaspoon cinnamon**
- **½ teaspoon salt**
- **1 cup butternut squash puree**
- **½ cup mini-marshmallows**

TOPPING
- **½ cup chopped pecans or walnuts**
- **¼ cup firmly packed light or dark brown sugar**
- **2 teaspoons cinnamon**

1 Preheat the oven to 350°F. Coat a 9-inch cake pan or 8x8-inch baking pan with cooking spray.

2 In a large mixing bowl or the bowl of an electric mixer, beat the sugar and margarine until creamy. Beat in 1 cup of the buttermilk or milk, the sour cream, egg, and vanilla. Add the flour, baking powder, cinnamon, and salt, and mix until completely incorporated.

3 Pour half of the batter into the pan and smooth the top. Spread the squash puree over the batter and sprinkle with marshmallows. Stir the remaining ¼ cup milk into the rest of the batter and spread evenly over the squash filling.

4 Mix together the topping ingredients and sprinkle evenly over the batter. Bake until a toothpick comes out clean when inserted into the center of the cake, 55 to 60 minutes. Let cool 5 minutes on a rack before cutting into wedges or squares.

Green Eggs
(WITH SPINACH)

Despite the eggs being green, I cannot believe how much my kids love these eggs. This quick meal doesn't require a puree, either.

Prep: 7 minutes • Total: 35 minutes • Serves 4

- 2 teaspoons trans-fat-free soft tub margarine spread
- 1 pound baby spinach, washed and drained
- 3 tablespoons lowfat milk
- 4 large eggs
- 2 large egg whites
- Pinch of salt
- Nonstick cooking spray
- Turkey bacon (optional)

1 Melt 1 teaspoon of the margarine in a large nonstick skillet over medium heat. Add the spinach, turn the heat to high, and cook, stirring often, until the spinach wilts. Then add the milk and cook to evaporate, 1 to 2 more minutes. Transfer to a food processor and puree; let cool a few minutes.

2 In a large bowl, whisk the eggs with the puree and the salt.

3 Coat the same skillet with cooking spray and set the pan over medium heat. Add the remaining teaspoon margarine and heat until melted. Add the egg mixture, reduce the heat to low, and cook, stirring occasionally, 2 to 3 minutes.

Sascha: *Wow! Green eggs? Can we make pink eggs next time?*

Jessica: *Hmm, maybe. . . . In the meantime, let's read* Green Eggs and Ham *by Dr. Seuss!*

Peanut Butter and Jelly Muffins

(WITH CARROT)

I don't know who likes these more, kids or grown-ups.

Prep: 10 minutes • Total: 35 minutes • Makes 12 muffins • Packable

- **Nonstick cooking spray**
- **½ cup natural peanut butter (creamy)**
- **½ cup carrot puree**
- **½ cup firmly packed light or dark brown sugar**
- **2 tablespoons trans-fat-free soft tub margarine spread**
- **½ cup nonfat plain yogurt**
- **1 large egg white**
- **1 cup all-purpose flour**
- **1 teaspoon baking powder**
- **1 teaspoon baking soda**
- **½ teaspoon salt**
- **½ cup low-sugar strawberry, blueberry, or grape preserves**

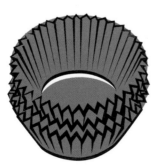

1 Preheat the oven to 350°F. Coat a 12-cup muffin tin with cooking spray or line with paper baking cups.

2 In a large bowl, beat the peanut butter, carrot puree, sugar, and margarine with a wooden spoon until well combined. Stir in the yogurt and egg white.

3 Add the flour, baking powder, baking soda, and salt. Stir until just combined, but do not overmix—there should be some lumps in the batter.

4 Divide the batter among the muffin cups and drop a spoonful of preserves on top of each.

5 Bake until the tops of the muffins are lightly browned and a toothpick comes out clean when inserted into the center, 20 to 25 minutes. Turn the muffins out onto a rack to cool.

6 Store in an airtight container at room temperature for up to 2 days, or wrap individually and freeze for up to 1 month.

(see top of photograph on next page)

Blueberry Lemon Muffins

(WITH YELLOW SQUASH)

Using an ice cream scoop to fill the muffin cups makes it easy!

Prep: 10 minutes • Total: 26 minutes • Makes 12 muffins • Packable

- **Nonstick cooking spray**
- **½ cup firmly packed light or dark brown sugar**
- **4 tablespoons trans-fat-free soft tub margarine spread, chilled**
- **1 cup lowfat lemon yogurt**
- **1 cup blueberries**
- **½ cup yellow squash puree**
- **1 large egg**
- **2 teaspoons pure lemon extract**
- **1 teaspoon grated lemon zest**
- **2 cups all-purpose flour**
- **¼ cup flaxseed meal**
- **1 teaspoon baking powder**
- **1 teaspoon baking soda**
- **½ teaspoon salt**

1 Preheat the oven to 350°F. Coat a 12-cup muffin tin with cooking spray or line with paper baking cups.

2 In a large bowl, beat the sugar and the margarine with a wooden spoon. Stir in the yogurt, blueberries, yellow squash puree, egg, lemon extract, and lemon zest.

3 Add the flour, flaxseed meal, baking powder, baking soda, and salt. Stir just to combine, but do not overmix—the batter is supposed to be lumpy.

4 Divide the batter among the muffin cups. Bake until the tops of the muffins are lightly browned and a toothpick comes out clean when inserted in the center, 13 to 16 minutes. Turn the muffins out onto a rack to cool.

5 Store in an airtight container at room temperature for up to 2 days, or wrap individually and freeze for up to 1 month.

(bottom of photograph, opposite)

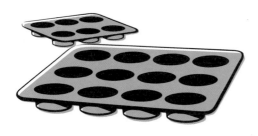

Baked Egg Puffs

(WITH YELLOW SQUASH OR BUTTERNUT SQUASH)

My children love these cute, puffy little egg soufflés. I make them in ramekins (or small coffee cups) so that we each get our own individual puff. One of these makes a full meal for a child whether for breakfast, lunch, or dinner.

Prep: 5 minutes • Total: 20 minutes • Serves 4

- **Nonstick cooking spray**
- **2 large eggs**
- **4 large egg whites**
- **½ cup yellow squash or butternut squash puree**
- **2 tablespoons shredded reduced-fat Cheddar cheese**
- **2 tablespoons all-purpose flour**
- **½ teaspoon baking powder**
- **¼ teaspoon salt**

1 Preheat the oven to 400°F. Coat 4 (½-cup) ramekins or coffee cups with cooking spray and set on a baking sheet.

2 In a large bowl, whisk the eggs, egg whites, squash puree, cheese, flour, baking powder, and salt until combined. Divide the mixture among the ramekins or cups and bake until the tops are puffed up and the eggs are no longer runny in the center when pierced with the tip of a knife, 13 to 15 minutes. Serve immediately.

Sascha: *Wow, I get my own little cup? Fun!*

Julian: *Mine is puffier than yours.*

Oatmeal

(WITH PUMPKIN OR SWEET POTATO)

You can also prepare this in the microwave for a hearty but healthy breakfast. Stir the ingredients into a microwave-safe bowl and cook for 2 minutes.

Prep: 10 minutes • Total: 13 minutes • Serves 2

- 1 cup nonfat (skim) milk
- ¼ cup firmly packed light or dark brown sugar
- ¼ cup canned pumpkin or sweet potato puree
- 1 teaspoon pure vanilla extract (optional)
- ¼ teaspoon cinnamon or pumpkin pie spice
- 1 cup old-fashioned oats
- 2 teaspoons natural peanut butter (optional)
- Dried fruit and nuts (optional)
- Pure maple syrup, for serving

1 In a small saucepan, combine the milk, sugar, pumpkin, vanilla, if using, and spice. Bring to a gentle boil and stir in the oatmeal. Reduce the heat and simmer for 2 to 3 minutes, until the oatmeal is soft and creamy. Stir in the peanut butter, if using.

2 Spoon the oatmeal into bowls, sprinkle with dried fruit and nuts, if you like, and serve warm with maple syrup.

Variation

Add 2 tablespoons of sweet potato to 1 cup of oatmeal. Next add ¼ cup of nonfat milk and ¼ cup of water. Add cinnamon to taste, and top with maple syrup or brown sugar.

Jessica: *Kids love to pour their own syrup out of a little plastic medicine cup, which comes with most over-the-counter children's medicines.*

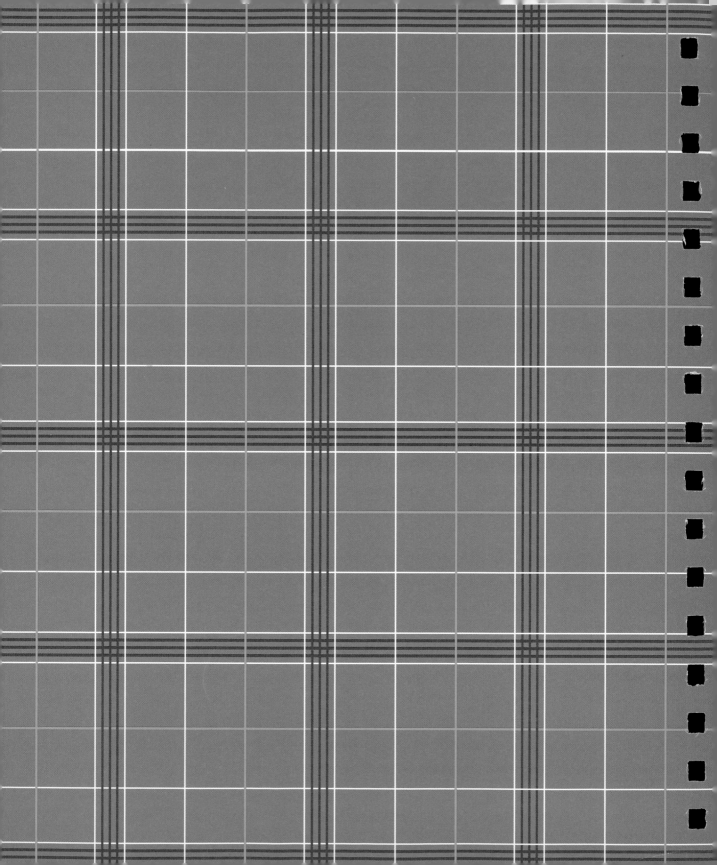

MEALTIME

Meatball Soup 72

Chicken Nuggets 75

Italian Meatloaf 79

Mashed Potatoes 80

Beef Stew 83

Chicken Salad 84

Rice Balls 87

Mozzarella Sticks 91

Homemade Ketchup 92

Aloha Chicken Kebabs 95

Pita Pizzas 96

Deviled Eggs 99

Tofu Nuggets 100

Chicken Alphabet Soup 103

Macaroni and Cheese 1 104

Macaroni and Cheese 2 107

"Buttered" Noodles 108

Burgers 1 111

Tuna Salad 112

Burgers 2 115

Spaghetti Pie 116

Pasta with Bolognese Sauce . . . 119

Spaghetti with Meatballs 120

Ranch Dressing 123

Greek Dip 123

Quesadillas 124

Salsa Dip 127

Creamy Potato Soup 128

Lasagna 131

Grilled Cheese Sandwiches 135

Avocado Spread 136

Twice-Baked Potatoes 139

Waffle Sandwiches 140

Pink Pancakes 143

Tortilla "Cigars" 144

Sloppy Joes 147

Tacos 148

Turkey Chili 151

Couscous 152

Meatball Soup

(WITH CARROT AND SWEET POTATO)

This is real comfort food. If I'm short on time or don't have vegetable purees, I finely chop the carrot and sweet potato, raw, in the food processor—it works just as well.

Prep: 20 minutes • Total: 35 minutes • Serves 10

- 3 ounces whole-wheat pasta shapes, such as bowties or wagon wheels
- Nonstick cooking spray
- 1 tablespoon olive oil
- 1 small onion, chopped
- 2 cloves garlic, chopped
- 1 (28-ounce) can whole peeled tomatoes, with their juice
- ¼ cup carrot puree
- 1½ teaspoons salt
- 3 cups reduced-fat low-sodium beef or chicken broth
- 3 slices whole-wheat bread, cubed
- 1 large egg, lightly beaten
- ¼ cup sweet potato puree
- ¼ cup nonfat (skim) milk
- 2 tablespoons grated Parmesan, plus more for serving
- ¼ teaspoon pepper
- ¼ teaspoon paprika
- ½ pound lean ground turkey

1 Cook the pasta in a large pot of boiling salted water according to package directions until al dente. Drain in a colander and set aside.

2 Coat a large pot with cooking spray and set it over medium-high heat. When the pot is hot, add the oil and then the onion and garlic. Cook, stirring often, until the onion is softened but not browned, 3 to 4 minutes.

3 Puree the tomatoes and their juice with the carrot puree in a food processor or blender, then add to the pot along with ½ teaspoon salt. Add the broth, reduce heat to low, and simmer, covered, for 10 to 15 minutes.

4 Meanwhile, put the bread in a large bowl. Add the egg, sweet potato puree, milk, Parmesan, 1 teaspoon salt, the pepper, and paprika, and let soak until the bread is very soft. Stir to break up the bread, add the ground turkey, and mix until smooth. Form into mini-meatballs ½-inch in diameter.

5 Add the meatballs to the pot. Simmer, covered, until the meatballs are no longer pink in the center, 12 to 15 minutes. Stir in the pasta. Serve sprinkled with Parmesan.

Chicken Nuggets

(WITH BROCCOLI OR SPINACH OR SWEET POTATO OR BEET)

I don't know any kid who doesn't like chicken nuggets. Just don't tell them what's hidden inside!

Prep: 10 minutes • Total: 20 minutes • Serves 4 • Packable

- 1 cup whole-wheat, white, or panko (Japanese) breadcrumbs
- ½ cup flaxseed meal
- 1 tablespoon grated Parmesan
- ½ teaspoon paprika
- ½ teaspoon garlic powder
- ½ teaspoon onion powder
- 1 cup broccoli or spinach or sweet potato or beet puree
- 1 large egg, lightly beaten
- 1 pound boneless, skinless chicken breast or chicken tenders, rinsed, dried, and cut into small chunks
- ½ teaspoon salt
- Nonstick cooking spray
- 1 tablespoon olive oil

1 In a bowl, combine the breadcrumbs, flaxseed meal, Parmesan, paprika, garlic, and onion powder on the paper or foil, and mix well with your fingers.

2 In a shallow bowl, mix the vegetable puree and egg with a fork and set the bowl next to the breadcrumb mixture.

3 Sprinkle the chicken chunks with the salt. Dip the chunks into the egg mixture and then toss them in the breadcrumbs until completely coated.

4 Coat a large nonstick skillet with cooking spray and set over medium-high heat. When the skillet is hot, add the oil. Place the chicken nuggets in the skillet in a single layer, being careful not to crowd the pan, and cook until crisp and golden on one side, 3 to 4 minutes. Then turn and cook until the chicken is cooked through, golden brown and crisp all over, 4 to 5 minutes longer. (Cut into a piece to check that it's cooked through.) Serve warm.

Variations

CHICKEN NUGGETS PARMESAN:

Use an ovenproof skillet to cook the breaded nuggets, then spoon 1 cup bottled tomato sauce over them and sprinkle with ½ cup shredded part-skim mozzarella. Bake for 10 minutes at 400°F to melt the cheese.

FISH NUGGETS:

Use 1 pound skinless, boneless salmon, tilapia, or other wild-caught mild fish, cut into small chunks, in place of the chicken. Coat and cook the fish exactly as you would the chicken, but reduce the cooking time to 2 to 3 minutes per side.

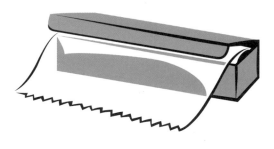

Joy: *When you make these nuggets with broccoli, your child will get the same amount of calcium as in 4 ounces of milk, plus more than 100% the daily value for vitamin C—particularly important for kids, since vitamin C may protect against colds and can help heal cuts and scrapes.*

Dining Out

When you have young kids, you are always looking for ways to reduce stress, and for me that means avoiding restaurants when I can. Mealtime should be for enjoyment, but that's hard when you're worried about making too much noise, telling your kids to sit down, or picking up dropped food off the floor. Most important, even in restaurants that have kids' menus, it's hard to find healthful food they will eat. When my kids are at home, at least I know they're getting good food.

Of course, you can't completely avoid eating out, especially when you are traveling or for special occasions. So on those rare days when we go out with our kids, we try to follow a few rules:

1 Try to go to a kid friendly spot—diners with booths are great options.

2 Order as you are seated—or as soon as possible thereafter.

3 Ask for the check as the food arrives so you aren't trying to find the waiter or waitress *after* your kids have lost their patience.

4 Avoid the kids' menu if you can. The standard hot dog, hamburger, and grilled cheese are usually much greasier and less nutritious than the adult entrees, which are great to split among two or more kids.

Italian Meatloaf

(WITH CARROT)

This is a perfect place to use a food processor to save time. Finely chopped raw carrot will work as well as puree.

Prep: 15 minutes • Total: 80–85 minutes • Serves 8 • Packable

- **Nonstick cooking spray**
- **1 cup Italian-style (seasoned) breadcrumbs**
- **½ cup nonfat (skim) milk**
- **2 tablespoons olive oil**
- **½ onion, finely chopped**
- **2 celery stalks, finely chopped**
- **1 pound lean ground turkey**
- **½ cup grated Parmesan**
- **½ cup carrot puree**
- **¼ cup ketchup**
- **1 teaspoon salt**
- **⅛ teaspoon pepper**
- **1 cup bottled tomato sauce**
- **4 slices turkey bacon**

1 Preheat the oven to 350°F. Coat a 9x5-inch loaf pan with cooking spray.

2 In a large bowl, soak the breadcrumbs in milk.

3 Coat a large nonstick skillet with cooking spray and set it over medium-high heat. When the skillet is hot, add the oil. Add the onion and cook, stirring occasionally, 7 to 10 minutes. Add the celery and cook 3 to 4 minutes longer. Scrape the mixture into the bowl with the breadcrumbs. Add the turkey, Parmesan, carrot puree, ketchup, salt, and pepper, and stir to combine.

4 Turn the mixture into the loaf pan and smooth the top. Spread tomato sauce over the meatloaf and lay the strips of bacon on top. Bake until the center of the meatloaf is no longer pink and the bacon begins to brown, 45 to 50 minutes. Cut into slices and serve.

Julian: I like a meatloaf sandwich!

Mashed Potatoes

(WITH CAULIFLOWER)

This recipe can be made with any type of potato, but baking potatoes make the fluffiest mashed potatoes.

Prep: 5 minutes • Total: 45 minutes • Serves 4

- **1 pound baking potatoes, peeled and cubed**
- **1 teaspoon salt**
- **½ cup cauliflower puree**
- **2 tablespoons trans-fat-free soft tub margarine spread**
- **½ cup lowfat (1%) buttermilk**

1 Put the potatoes and salt in a large pot and add enough water to cover the potatoes by about 3 inches. Bring to a boil over high heat, then reduce the heat and simmer until the potatoes are tender when pierced with a fork, 15 to 20 minutes. (Or steam them for about 30 minutes.) Drain well in a colander.

2 Set a potato ricer over the pot and pass the potatoes through in batches. (Or return potatoes to the pot and mash with a potato masher.) Add the cauliflower puree, margarine, and buttermilk, and beat with a large spoon until the potatoes are smooth and creamy.

Shepherd: *Mmmm . . . good!*

Keep On Schedule

ITRY TO AVOID mood swings and hunger-induced crankiness in my kids by being as disciplined with myself about schedules as my life with young children will permit. It's hard to do, but I've found that my kids' moods become more predictable when they are fed on time. I know how I get when I'm hungry! So I keep their mealtimes as close as possible to the same time every day, and try to make sure that meals and snacks fall no more than $2\frac{1}{2}$ or 3 hours apart.

Our Mealtime Schedule

Breakfast at 7:00 A.M.

Morning snack at 10:00 A.M.

Lunch at 12:30 P.M.

Afternoon snack at 3:00 P.M.

Dinner at 5:30 P.M.

Beef Stew

(WITH BROCCOLI)

Before serving to kids, I shred the cooked beef with a wooden spoon and then serve the whole thing over pasta or rice. For adults, you can leave the beef nice and chunky.

Prep: 25 minutes • Total: 5½ hours • Serves 8 to 10

- **1 medium onion, quartered**
- **2 medium carrots, cut into large chunks**
- **2 stalks celery, cut into large chunks**
- **2 cloves garlic, crushed**
- **3 pounds boneless beef stew meat, cut into 1-inch cubes**
- **⅓ cup all-purpose flour**
- **1 teaspoon salt**
- **¼ teaspoon pepper**
- **Nonstick cooking spray**
- **1 tablespoon olive oil**
- **3 cups reduced-fat low-sodium beef broth**
- **1 (15-ounce) can chopped tomatoes, with their juice**
- **1 large potato, any kind, peeled and cut into ½-inch cubes**
- **½ cup broccoli puree**

1 Toss the onion, carrots, celery, and garlic into the food processor and process until finely chopped; set aside.

2 In a large zipper-lock bag or a bowl, toss the beef with the flour, salt, and pepper until evenly coated.

3 Coat a large nonstick skillet with cooking spray and set it over medium-high heat. When the pan is hot, add the oil, then add half of the beef and brown it on all sides for 3 to 4 minutes. Transfer to a large pot. Cook the rest of the beef the same way and add it to the pot.

4 Add the chopped onion, carrot, celery, and garlic to the skillet, reduce the heat to medium, and cook for 6 to 7 minutes, or until the vegetables begin to soften. Add them to the pot.

5 Add the beef broth, tomatoes and their juice, and broccoli puree, cover, and bring to a boil, then reduce the heat and simmer 4 hours. Add the potatoes and cook until the meat is very tender and begins to fall apart, 4½ to 5 hours total.

Chicken Salad

(WITH CAULIFLOWER)

Children love grapes, so this makes a great lunch for the whole family. Using leftover roast chicken saves time; so does using a food processor to chop the celery.

Prep: 20 minutes • Total: 45 minutes • Serves 4

- **2 large eggs**
- **1 pound boneless, skinless chicken cutlets or breast, rinsed and dried**
- **1 teaspoon salt**
- **¼ teaspoon chili powder, or to taste**
- **¼ teaspoon sweet paprika**
- **¼ teaspoon garlic powder**
- **Nonstick cooking spray**
- **1 teaspoon olive oil**
- **¾ cup reduced-fat mayonnaise**
- **2 stalks celery, finely chopped (about ¾ cup)**
- **½ cup cauliflower puree**
- **½ cup nonfat plain yogurt**
- **½ cup green grapes, coarsely chopped**

1 Place the eggs in a small saucepan and add cold water to cover. Cover, set the saucepan over high heat, and bring to a boil, then remove from the heat and let stand, still covered, for exactly 15 minutes. Run the eggs under cold water to cool, then peel them. Separate the yolks from the whites. Chop the whites and discard the yolks (or refrigerate for another use).

2 Sprinkle the chicken with salt, chili powder, paprika, and garlic powder. Coat a large nonstick skillet with cooking spray and set it over medium-high heat. When the skillet is hot, add the oil and then the chicken. For cutlets, cook 4 to 5 minutes per side until lightly browned and no longer pink in the center. For chicken breast, cook 5 minutes per side, reduce the heat to low, cover, and cook for 9 to 10 minutes longer. Let the chicken cool slightly before cutting it into bite-sized pieces.

3 In a large bowl, stir together the chicken, mayonnaise, celery, cauliflower puree, yogurt, grapes, and chopped egg whites. Serve warm or chilled.

Rice Balls

(WITH SWEET POTATO AND SPINACH OR BROCCOLI OR BUTTERNUT SQUASH)

Spraying these cute little round balls with cooking spray a few times while they brown gives them a crisp, "deep-fried" crust without the deep-frying. If you leave out the chicken, the rice balls make a great meal for vegetarians.

Prep: 30 minutes • Total: 40 minutes • Serves 6 to 8 (about 40 rice balls)

- ½ cup short-grain brown rice (or 1 cup leftover cooked rice)
- Nonstick cooking spray
- 3 teaspoons olive oil
- ¼ pound chicken cutlets, rinsed and dried
- 1¼ teaspoons salt
- ⅛ teaspoon pepper
- ½ cup sweet potato puree
- ¼ cup shredded reduced-fat Cheddar cheese
- ¼ cup lowfat (1%) buttermilk
- 1 large egg, lightly beaten
- ½ cup spinach or broccoli or butternut squash puree
- 1½ cups whole-wheat cracker crumbs or breadcrumbs

1 Place the rice in a small saucepan with 1 cup of water; cover and bring to a boil. Reduce the heat to very low and cook until the rice is tender, 30 to 40 minutes. You can also use your rice steamer.

2 Meanwhile, coat a large nonstick skillet with cooking spray and set it over medium-high heat. When the pan is hot, add 1 teaspoon oil. Sprinkle the chicken with ¼ teaspoon salt and the pepper, and cook until no longer pink in the center, 4 to 5 minutes per side.

3 Cut the chicken into chunks and place them in a food processor or blender. Add the sweet potato puree, cheese, 1 teaspoon salt, and the buttermilk, and blend until smooth. Transfer the mixture to a large bowl and stir in the cooked rice. Roll the mixture into 1-inch balls and place them on a sheet of waxed paper or aluminum foil.

4 In a shallow bowl, beat the egg and vegetable puree with a fork. Put the crumbs in the bowl. One at a time, dip the rice balls in the egg mixture, then roll them in the crumbs to make an even coating.

5 Coat a large nonstick skillet with cooking spray and set it over medium-high heat. When the pan is hot, add the remaining 2 teaspoons oil. Add the rice balls and cook for 5 to 7 minutes, turning occasionally and spraying with cooking spray, until browned and crisp all over. Serve warm.

My Dinner Program

AFTER STRUGGLING through several irritating phases when the children would eat only the pasta on their plates and ignore the vegetables and protein accompaniments, I hit upon the idea of serving separate courses so that the kids don't just focus in on one food and leave the rest.

1 While I am making the meal, I put crudités on the table with small dishes of lowfat sour cream or Greek Dip (page 123)—the kids dip and munch.

2 Next, I serve the chicken, fish, or tofu nuggets.

3 Once they've had a few bites, then comes a veggie side dish, such as steamed broccoli, carrots, or peas (and I quietly pray they will eat them).

4 Then comes the pasta or rice, because this is the easy part of the meal at our house.

Mozzarella Sticks

(WITH CAULIFLOWER)

I still can't believe I make mozzarella sticks at home—they always seemed like too much work. These are so easy, and the cheese hides the cauliflower puree entirely.

Prep: 20 minutes • Total: 45 minutes • Makes 8 mozzarella sticks • No meat

- **1 cup whole-wheat breadcrumbs**
- **1 tablespoon flaxseed meal**
- **1 tablespoon sesame seeds (optional)**
- **1 cup shredded part-skim mozzarella**
- **½ cup cauliflower puree**
- **1 tablespoon cornstarch**
- **Nonstick cooking spray**
- **1 tablespoon olive oil**
- **¼ teaspoon salt**

1 In a bowl, toss the breadcrumbs with the flaxseed meal and sesame seeds.

2 In a second large bowl, stir together the mozzarella, cauliflower puree, and cornstarch until well combined. Shape into eight 2x½-inch logs. Gently roll each log in the breadcrumbs, then wrap in aluminum foil or waxed paper and freeze for 20 minutes.

3 Coat a large nonstick skillet with cooking spray and set it over medium-high heat. When the pan is hot, add the oil. Arrange the mozzarella sticks in the pan in a single layer, being careful not to crowd them. Cook for 3 to 4 minutes, turning occasionally, until the crumb coating begins to brown. Sprinkle with salt and serve with ketchup.

Joy: *Lowfat cheese is actually a better source of calcium by volume than full-fat, because removing the fat makes room for more calcium-rich dairy.*

Homemade Ketchup

(WITH CARROT)

Doesn't every kid love ketchup?

Prep: 5 minutes • Total: 25 minutes • Makes 1 cup

- 1 (6-ounce) can tomato paste
- ½ cup carrot puree
- ¼ cup water
- 2 tablespoons apple-cider vinegar
- 2 cloves garlic, minced
- 1 tablespoon firmly packed light or dark brown sugar (optional)
- ½ teaspoon dry mustard
- ¼ teaspoon salt
- ¼ teaspoon ground allspice
- ¼ teaspoon chili powder, or to taste

1 Stir all the ingredients together in a big saucepan and bring to a boil over medium-high heat. Reduce the heat and simmer until the mixture has reduced by about half, 15 to 20 minutes. Let cool before serving.

2 Refrigerate in an airtight container for up to 5 days, or freeze in ¼-cup amounts in zipper-lock snack bags for up to 3 months.

(OTHER) MOTHERS KNOW BEST
(PART 2)

"When I boil Olivia's veggies, I boil them with an organic chicken boullion cube for a minute. The veggies are crunchy but have a little flavor of chicken and salt. She loves the way they taste (and won't eat them otherwise!) Or I sprinkle the veggies with a little olive oil and salt and bake them at 350°F for 15 minutes."

— Christina, Los Angeles
MOTHER OF OLIVIA, 5 AND GRIFFIN, 1

"Jacob really likes salad dressing, but won't touch salad. We give him cucumbers (don't ask me why he chooses cucumbers!) that he can dip in dressing. That seems to work like a charm. He also likes soy sauce, so if I sauté spinach in soy sauce with loads of lemon, he will eat that on occasion. Charlie will eat broccoli tops dipped in soy sauce, and they both like some honey on apples."

—Tina, San Francisco
MOTHER OF JACOB, 8, AND CHARLIE, 5

"Jackson will not eat a vegetable. I've tried buttering them up, salting them up, and even adding brown sugar. Nothing works. I have resorted to juicing, which he will drink. Fresh carrot juice with an apple and a small beet thrown in. I will keep trying the 'real' thing. He'll eat them someday—I hope!"

—Lorna, New York City
MOTHER OF JACKSON, 3

Aloha Chicken Kebabs

(WITH SWEET POTATO AND PINEAPPLE)

Crunchy and sweet—an unbeatable combination for kids. You can leave out the coconut if your kids don't like it, but once the chicken is cooked, the coconut is very hard to see.

Prep: 15 minutes • Total: 25 minutes • Serves 4 • Packable

- **1 cup whole-wheat breadcrumbs**
- **¼ cup flaxseed meal**
- ½ cup sweet potato puree
- ¼ cup pineapple puree
- **1 tablespoon reduced-sodium soy sauce**
- **1 large egg white, lightly beaten**
- **¼ cup shredded unsweetened coconut**
- **1 pound boneless, skinless chicken breast or chicken tenders, rinsed, dried, and cut into "fingers"**
- **¼ teaspoon salt**
- **2 tablespoons all-purpose or whole-wheat flour**
- **Nonstick cooking spray**
- **1 tablespoon olive oil**
- **10 to 12 short wooden skewers**

1 In a bowl, mix the breadcrumbs with the flaxseed meal. Set aside.

2 In a second wide, shallow bowl, combine the sweet potato and pineapple purees, soy sauce, egg white, and coconut, and mix with a fork; set next to the breadcrumbs.

3 Thread the chicken fingers lengthwise onto skewers, using one skewer per chicken finger. Sprinkle both sides of the chicken skewers with salt and then with flour. Dip the chicken into the egg-white mixture and then roll it in the breadcrumbs until completely coated.

4 Coat a large nonstick skillet with cooking spray and set it over medium-high heat. When the pan is hot, add the oil.

5 Add the chicken in a single layer and brown for 3 to 4 minutes on one side, until the breadcrumb coating is crisp and golden. (Turn down the heat if the coating browns too quickly—coconut burns easily.) Turn the skewers and cook 4 to 5 minutes longer, until the chicken is cooked through and browned all over.

Pita Pizzas

(WITH SPINACH)

This meal takes only about 3 minutes of actual work, and my kids love getting their own personal pizza. If I have leftover Bolognese sauce, I use that in place of the tomato sauce.

Prep: 3 minutes • Total: 18 minutes • Makes 8 mini-pizzas • No meat

- **8 (4-inch) whole-wheat pita pockets**
- ½ cup spinach puree
- **2 cups bottled tomato sauce**
- **2 cups thinly sliced part-skim mozzarella**

1 Preheat the oven to 400°F.

2 Spread spinach puree on each pita so that the spinach comes to within about ½ inch of the edge. Spread the sauce over the spinach; it should cover the spinach and come to within about ¼ inch of the edge of the pita. Now lay the cheese over the sauce, covering any place where the green comes through.

3 Place the pizzas on a foil-lined baking sheet and bake until the cheese melts and begins to brown, 5 to 10 minutes. Let the pizzas cool 5 minutes before serving so the cheese cools and doesn't pull off (and the spinach stays completely invisible).

Joy: *The spinach puree in these baby pizzas provides your child with a hearty dose of beta carotene, plus 3 grams of fiber. Tomato sauce adds lycopene (a potent antioxidant that helps to enhance overall health).*

Deviled Eggs

(WITH CAULIFLOWER OR CARROT)

This revamped classic looks and tastes just like the original, but it's so much better for your kids.

Prep and serve: 25 minutes • Serves 6 • Packable

- **6 large eggs**
- **3 tablespoons reduced-fat mayonnaise**
- **¼ cup cauliflower or carrot puree**
- **⅛ teaspoon salt**
- **pepper and paprika to taste and for presentation (optional)**

1 Place the eggs in a saucepan and add cold water to cover. Set the saucepan over high heat, cover, and bring the water to a boil. Immediately remove the pan from the heat and let stand, still covered, for exactly 15 minutes. Drain the eggs, cool under cold running water, and peel.

2 Cut eggs in half lengthwise and remove the yolks. Put three of the yolks in a bowl and discard the rest (or save for another meal).

3 Add the mayonnaise, vegetable puree, and salt, and mash together with a fork.

4 Fill each egg half with the yolk mixture.

Julian: *Mmm, I like the white part.*
Sascha: *I like the yellow part.*
Shepherd: *I like the whole thing.*

Tofu Nuggets

(WITH SPINACH OR BROCCOLI OR PEAS)

Think your kids won't touch tofu? When I serve these, my kids think they're eating chicken or cheese.

Prep: 15 minutes • Total: 25 minutes • Serves 4 • Packable • Meatless

- **1 cup whole-wheat or white breadcrumbs**
- **1 tablespoon flaxseed meal**
- **1 tablespoon grated Parmesan**
- **½ teaspoon paprika**
- **1 cup spinach or broccoli or pea puree**
- **1 large egg, lightly beaten**
- **1 (14-ounce) package extra-firm tofu (preferably with calcium)**
- **½ teaspoon salt**
- **Nonstick cooking spray**
- **1 tablespoon olive oil**

1 In a bowl, stir together the breadcrumbs, flaxseed meal, Parmesan, and paprika. Set aside.

2 In a shallow bowl, mix the spinach puree and egg with a fork, and set the bowl next to the breadcrumb mixture.

3 Slice the tofu ½-inch thick and cube it or cut into shapes with a cookie cutter. Sprinkle both sides with salt. Dip the tofu pieces into the puree mixture, then roll them in the breadcrumbs until the tofu is completely coated and you can't see the puree.

4 Coat a large nonstick skillet with cooking spray and set it over medium-high heat. When the pan is hot, add the oil.

5 Add the tofu nuggets in a single layer (be careful not to crowd the pan!) and cook until nicely browned on one side, 3 to 4 minutes. Turn and cook until the crumb coating is crisp and golden, 2 to 3 minutes longer.

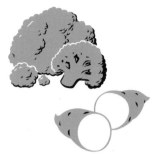

Chicken Alphabet Soup

(WITH CAULIFLOWER AND SWEET POTATO)

This is not much harder than opening a can! If your kids don't like whole bits of chicken, puree it before adding it to the soup—they'll never know it's there. And this is a good place to use up leftover roast chicken.

Prep and serve: 45 minutes • Serves 8

- **3 quarts reduced-fat low-sodium chicken broth**
- **1 chicken breast on the bone (about ½ pound), rinsed and dried, skin removed**
- **½ teaspoon salt**
- **½ cup alphabet pasta**
- **¼ cup cauliflower puree**
- **¼ cup sweet potato puree**

1 Bring the broth to a boil in a large pot. Sprinkle the chicken all over with the salt, then carefully slide it into the broth. Immediately turn off the heat, cover the pot, and allow to rest off the heat until the chicken is cooked through, 25 to 30 minutes.

2 Remove the chicken with a slotted spoon and let it cool on a plate for 3 to 4 minutes, until it's cool enough to handle easily. Then pull the meat off the bone (discard the bone), cut into bite-sized pieces, and set aside.

3 Bring the broth back to a simmer and add the pasta. Stir in the cauliflower and sweet potato purees and simmer for 5 to 6 minutes, or until the pasta is cooked. Stir in the chicken and serve hot.

Joy: *Sweet potato and cauliflower purees provide kids with vitamins A and C—good for vision, skin, and healthy immune systems.*

Macaroni and Cheese 1

(WITH BUTTERNUT SQUASH OR CAULIFLOWER)

I leave a box of store-bought macaroni and cheese out on the counter and the kids naturally assume. . . .

Prep: 5 minutes • Total: 25 minutes • Serves 4 • Packable

- 1½ cups elbow macaroni
- Nonstick cooking spray
- 1 tablespoon olive oil
- 1 tablespoon all-purpose flour
- ½ cup nonfat (skim) milk
- ½ cup butternut squash or cauliflower puree
- 1½ cups shredded reduced-fat Cheddar cheese (about 8 ounces)
- 4 ounces (almost ¼ cup) reduced-fat or nonfat cream cheese
- ½ teaspoon salt
- ⅛ teaspoon paprika
- ⅛ teaspoon pepper

1 Bring a large pot of salted water to a boil, add the macaroni, and cook according to package directions until al dente. Drain in a colander.

2 While the macaroni is cooking, coat a large saucepan with cooking spray and heat over medium heat. Add the oil, then the flour, and cook, stirring constantly, until the mixture resembles a thick paste but has not browned, 1 to 2 minutes.

3 Add the milk and cook, stirring every now and then, until the mixture begins to thicken, 3 to 4 minutes. Add the vegetable puree, Cheddar, cream cheese, and seasonings, and stir until the cheese is melted and the sauce is smooth. Stir in the macaroni and serve warm.

Joy: *This is a great source of calcium: one portion provides a full serving—the equivalent of one cup of milk. And because it uses lowfat cheese, kids get all that great calcium without the saturated fat of the traditional recipe.*

Pack-a-Snack

IKNOW IT SOUNDS annoying, but I send my children on play dates with snacks to share with their friends; it's a matter of self-preservation. Too often my kids have come home cranky—either from sugary snacks or no snacks at all. Now I ask my children to suggest a snack they think their friends might like. They choose whatever lunch box or bag they think is cool at the moment (they also like to color and put stickers on brown paper bags) and together we pack it full of the chosen treat. It comes home empty every time.

SOME OF MY FAMILY'S FAVORITE SNACKS:

- *Apple slices sprinkled with a little lemon juice (so they don't turn brown)*
- *Mozzarella or Cheddar cheese sticks*
- *Healthful muffins (pp. 50, 58, 61, 63)*
- *Cucumber or carrot sticks*
- *Banana bread (p. 54)*
- *Chocolate chip cookies (p. 177)*

MY FRIENDS WHO ARE PARENTS ALSO HAD THESE IDEAS:

- *Lowfat Cheddar cheese crackers*
- *Rolled slices of reduced-fat cheese or turkey breast*
- *Raisins, cranberries, and other dried fruits mixed with sunflower seeds*
- *Gorilla Munch*
- *Sliced English cucumber with salt*
- *Pistachios and walnuts*
- *Watermelon cubes*
- *Organic granola*
- *Peanut butter (with sliced apple or banana, or rice cakes)*
- *Frozen grapes*
- *Soy Crisps*
- *Vegetable chips*
- *Cheerios—MultiGrain, Honey Nut, or plain*
- *Low-sugar yogurts and yogurt tubes (freeze them so they are less messy). I like Stonyfield Farms brand.*
- *Organic fruit leather (without dyes or added sugar)*
- *Whole-wheat fig bars*
- *Oat-bran pretzels*
- *Whole-wheat frozen waffles*
- *Lowfat graham crackers*
- *Pita chips*

Macaroni and Cheese 2

(WITH BEANS)

Whatever light-colored canned beans you have on hand—chickpeas, navy beans, or white beans—will add a little more protein to the traditional recipe. For an extra boost of nutrition, add ½ cup of cauliflower puree along with the cheese.

Prep: 5 minutes • Total: 25 minutes • Serves 8 • Packable • No meat

- 1½ cups whole-wheat elbow macaroni
- 1 cup nonfat (skim) milk
- ½ cup canned navy beans or chickpeas or white beans, rinsed, drained, and pureed
- Nonstick cooking spray
- 1½ cups shredded reduced-fat Cheddar cheese (about 8 ounces)
- ½ teaspoon salt
- ⅛ teaspoon garlic powder
- ⅛ teaspoon paprika
- ⅛ teaspoon pepper

1 Bring a large pot of salted water to a boil, add the macaroni, and cook according to package directions until al dente. Drain in a colander.

2 While the macaroni is cooking, combine the milk and the beans in a food processor and process until pureed.

3 Coat a large saucepan with cooking spray and set it over medium heat. Add the bean mixture to the pan and cook, stirring until smooth, 1 to 2 minutes. Add the cheese and cook until melted and creamy, 1 to 2 minutes longer. Stir in the salt, garlic powder, paprika, and pepper. Stir in the macaroni and serve warm.

Jerry: I can't believe there are beans in here. This tastes great.

"Buttered" Noodles

(WITH YELLOW SQUASH)

Simple buttered noodles make most kids very happy. In this version, they're getting their veggies, too.

Prep: 5 minutes • Total: 25 minutes • Serves 4 • No meat

- **8 ounces whole-wheat spaghetti, angel hair, or other pasta**
- **½ cup yellow squash puree**
- **¼ cup nonfat (skim) milk**
- **2 tablespoons trans-fat-free soft tub margarine spread**
- **2 tablespoons grated Parmesan**
- **¼ teaspoon salt**

1 Bring a large pot of salted water to a boil. Add the pasta and cook according to package directions until al dente.

2 Drain, return the pasta to the warm pot, and stir in the squash puree (make sure the puree is very creamy), milk, margarine, Parmesan, and salt.

Jessica: *To save time, while the pasta cooks, you can boil vegetables you may want to serve as a side dish, such as carrots or broccoli or string beans, in the pasta water.*

Burgers 1

(WITH CAULIFLOWER OR CARROT)

If you're short on time, skip the puree and just finely chop raw cauliflower or carrot in the food processor.

Prep: 10 minutes • Total: 20 minutes • Makes 8 little burgers, serves 4

- ½ **pound lean ground turkey or sirloin**
- ½ **cup breadcrumbs**
- ½ cup cauliflower or carrot puree
- ¼ **cup nonfat (skim) milk**
- **2 tablespoons low-sodium soy sauce**
- **2 cloves garlic, chopped**
- ⅛ **teaspoon pepper**
- **Nonstick cooking spray**
- **1 tablespoon olive oil**
- **8 small whole-grain dinner rolls or whole-grain bread slices, for serving**

1 Preheat the oven to 400°F.

2 In a large bowl, stir together the meat, breadcrumbs, vegetable puree, milk, soy sauce, garlic, and pepper with a wooden spoon; the mixture will be moist. Form it into 8 small patties and place them on a sheet of waxed paper or aluminum foil.

3 Coat a large nonstick ovenproof skillet with cooking spray and set it over medium-high heat. When the skillet is hot, add the oil. Add the burgers and cook until nicely browned on one side, 4 to 5 minutes. Turn the burgers, then slide the skillet into the oven and bake for 4 to 5 minutes longer, until the burgers are no longer pink in the center. Serve each burger on a split roll.

Sascha: *Shepherd doesn't like meat, so he won't eat these. But we love them, right Julian?*

Julian: *Right!*

Tuna Salad

(WITH CAULIFLOWER)

While this dish looks nice served on top of lettuce leaves, my children would scream at the sight of lettuce. Instead, I serve it on whole wheat bread or stuffed into pita.

Prep and serve: 5–8 minutes • Serves 4

- 2 (6-ounce) cans light tuna packed in spring water
- ½ cup cauliflower puree
- ¼ cup reduced-fat mayonnaise
- 2 stalks celery, finely chopped or grated (about ¾ cup)
- ¼ teaspoon chili powder, or to taste
- ¼ teaspoon sweet paprika
- ¼ teaspoon garlic powder
- ½ teaspoon salt, or to taste
- ⅛ teaspoon pepper

1 Drain the tuna well, then turn it into a large bowl and break it up with a fork.

2 Fold in the cauliflower puree and mayonnaise. Then stir in the celery and seasonings.

Joy: One serving of this salad provides 21 grams of lean, high-quality protein and a good amount of B vitamins (important for healthy immune systems). Make the salad with light rather than white tuna, because white tuna has been shown to contain high levels of mercury.

Burgers 2

(WITH MUSHROOMS AND ZUCCHINI)

If you can't find whole-grain hamburger buns, make your own by using a glass to cut out rounds from whole-wheat bread slices. Use a mini- or regular-sized food processor to make quick work of chopping the mushrooms and zucchini.

Prep: 15 minutes • Total: 35 minutes • Makes 16 little burgers

- **1 pound lean ground turkey or sirloin**
- **½ pound white button or (stemmed) shiitake mushrooms, trimmed and finely chopped**
- **1 cup whole-wheat or Italian (seasoned) breadcrumbs**
- **¼ cup chopped or grated zucchini**
- **1 tablespoon Worcestershire sauce**
- **2 tablespoons ketchup**
- **½ teaspoon salt**
- **⅛ teaspoon pepper**
- **Nonstick cooking spray**
- **1 tablespoon olive oil**
- **16 whole-grain hamburger buns, for serving**

1 Preheat the oven to 400°F.

2 In a large bowl, mix the meat, mushrooms, breadcrumbs, zucchini, Worcestershire sauce, ketchup, salt, and pepper until well combined. The mixture will be moist. Form into 16 patties and place them on a sheet of waxed paper or aluminum foil.

3 Coat a large nonstick ovenproof skillet with cooking spray and set it over medium-high heat. When the skillet is hot, add the oil. Add the burgers and brown on one side for 4 to 5 minutes. Turn the burgers, then slide the skillet into the oven. Bake for 4 to 5 minutes longer, or until the burgers are no longer pink in the center. Serve each burger on a bun.

Jerry: *I don't ask what's in these, either.*

Spaghetti Pie

(WITH BROCCOLI AND CARROT)

This is a perfect recipe for that leftover pasta you've got in the fridge from last night's dinner.

Prep: 20 minutes • Total: 45 minutes • Serves 8 to 10

- **Nonstick cooking spray**
- **3 ounces whole-wheat spaghetti or angel hair pasta (or 1 cup leftover cooked pasta)**
- **½ pound lean ground turkey or sirloin**
- **½ cup broccoli puree**
- **1 large egg white**
- **2 tablespoons grated Parmesan**
- **2 cloves garlic, chopped**
- **2 cups bottled tomato sauce**
- **1 cup lowfat (1%) cottage cheese**
- **¼ cup carrot puree**
- **½ teaspoon salt**
- **¼ teaspoon pepper**
- **1 cup shredded part-skim mozzarella**

1 Preheat the oven to 350°F. Coat a 9-inch pie plate with cooking spray.

2 Bring a large pot of salted water to a boil, add the pasta, and cook until al dente. Drain in a colander. (Skip this step if you have leftover pasta.)

3 In a small bowl, mix the ground turkey or sirloin with the broccoli puree, egg white, Parmesan, and garlic. Form the mixture into ½-inch balls.

4 In a large bowl, stir the cooked pasta, tomato sauce, cottage cheese, carrot puree, and salt and pepper. Spoon the mixture into the pie plate and smooth the top. Scatter meatballs on top and sprinkle with mozzarella. Bake, uncovered, until the center is firm and the cheese is bubbly, 25 to 30 minutes.

Sascha: *This reminds me of pizza, but it's made with spaghetti.*

Julian: *The crust is so crunchy!*

But I'm Starving!

WHAT TO DO with the kids who wander into the kitchen, hungry for dinner, while you're still cooking?

About 15 minutes before serving dinner, I put a plate of raw veggies on the table for nibblers and direct hungry children to it (I do the same with berries before breakfast). This way, I'm confident that I've addressed their complaint and there's something healthful to eat if they're truly hungry (and not just bored). They now happily devour carrots and celery every night. And believe me, this wasn't always the case! If they eat all the veggies and only nibble at their dinner, that's fine with me too because I know they've gotten a first course of vegetables.

Pasta with Bolognese Sauce

(WITH SWEET POTATO)

This recipe makes twice as much sauce as you need to serve pasta for 4; freeze the rest for another meal. Finely chopped raw sweet potato may be substituted for puree.

Prep: 15 minutes • Total: 45 minutes • Serves 4

- 1 medium onion, finely chopped
- 2 cloves garlic, finely chopped
- Nonstick cooking spray
- 1 tablespoon olive oil
- 3 carrots
- 1 stalk celery
- ½ pound lean ground sirloin
- ½ pound lean ground turkey
- ½ teaspoon salt
- ⅛ teaspoon pepper
- 1 large (26-ounce) can crushed tomatoes
- 1 (8-ounce) can reduced-fat low-sodium chicken or beef broth
- 1 tablespoon sugar
- ½ cup sweet potato puree
- 2 tablespoons grated Parmesan
- 1 pound any pasta, preferably whole wheat or whole grain

1 Put the onion and garlic in the food processor and finely chop (or chop by hand).

2 Coat a large nonstick skillet with cooking spray and set it over medium-high heat. When the skillet is hot, add the oil, then the onion and garlic, and cook until the onion begins to soften, 2 to 3 minutes.

3 Meanwhile, put the carrot and celery in the food processor and finely chop; add to the skillet and cook 3 to 4 minutes longer.

4 Increase the heat to high, add the ground meats, and break them into small chunks with a wooden spoon. Add the salt and pepper and cook until the meat begins to brown, 3 to 4 minutes. Add the tomatoes, broth, and sugar. Reduce the heat to low, cover, and simmer, stirring occasionally, for 30 minutes. Stir in the sweet potato puree and Parmesan.

5 Cook the pasta in a large pot of salted boiling water according to package directions until al dente. Drain in a colander, then return the pasta to the pot. Pour the warm sauce over the pasta and toss.

Spaghetti and Meatballs

(WITH BUTTERNUT SQUASH AND CARROT)

Leftover meatballs are great to pack for school lunches. You can finely chop raw butternut squash and carrot if you're low on purees.

Prep: 20 minutes • Total: 45 minutes • Serves 6

- ½ pound lean ground turkey
- 1 cup breadcrumbs
- ½ cup butternut squash puree
- 1 clove garlic, minced
- 1 teaspoon salt
- ¼ plus ⅛ teaspoon black pepper
- Nonstick cooking spray
- 2 teaspoons olive oil
- 1 (26-ounce) can whole peeled tomatoes with their juice, pureed in a blender
- ½ cup water
- ¼ cup carrot puree (optional)
- ¼ teaspoon garlic powder
- Pinch of cayenne pepper
- 1 bay leaf
- 1 pound spaghetti or angel hair pasta, preferably whole wheat or whole grain

1 In a large bowl, mix the turkey, breadcrumbs, butternut squash puree, garlic, ½ teaspoon salt, and ¼ teaspoon black pepper until well combined. Shape the mixture into 1-inch meatballs and place on a sheet of waxed paper or aluminum foil.

2 Coat a large nonstick skillet with cooking spray and set it over high heat. When the skillet is hot, add the olive oil and then the meatballs and brown for 4 to 5 minutes, turning occasionally.

3 Add the pureed tomatoes, water, carrot puree (if using), garlic powder, cayenne, bay leaf, and the remaining ½ teaspoon salt and ⅛ teaspoon pepper. Reduce the heat to low and simmer for 15 to 20 minutes, or until the meatballs are no longer pink in the center. Remove the bay leaf.

4 Meanwhile, bring a large pot of salted water to a boil. Add the pasta and cook according to package directions until al dente. Drain the pasta in a colander, turn it into a serving bowl, and spoon the meatballs and sauce over it.

Ranch Dressing

(WITH NAVY OR GREAT NORTHERN BEANS)

Total: 5 minutes • Makes 1½ cups

- **1 cup lowfat (1%) buttermilk**
- 1 cup canned navy or Great Northern beans, drained, rinsed, and mashed
- **2 tablespoons reduced-fat sour cream**
- **1 clove garlic, chopped**
- **1 tablespoon grated Parmesan**
- **1 tablespoon dried parsley flakes**
- **½ teaspoon salt**
- **¼ teaspoon pepper**
- **⅛ teaspoon chili powder, or to taste**

Combine the buttermilk, beans, sour cream, garlic, Parmesan, and seasonings in a blender or mini-chopper and process until smooth. Serve immediately or refrigerate in a tightly covered container for up to 3 days.

Greek Dip

(WITH CHICKPEAS AND ARTICHOKES)

Total: 5 minutes • Serves 4

- 1 cup each canned chickpeas and chopped artichoke hearts, drained and rinsed
- **½ cup reduced-fat mayonnaise**
- **2 tablespoons grated Parmesan**
- **2 tablespoons lemon juice**
- **1 clove garlic, crushed**
- **½ teaspoon salt**
- **¼ teaspoon chili powder, or to taste**
- **⅛ teaspoon pepper**
- **⅛ teaspoon onion powder**

In a food processor, process the chickpeas until chopped. Add the artichoke hearts, mayonnaise, Parmesan, lemon juice, garlic, and seasonings, and blend until pureed.

Quesadillas

(WITH BUTTERNUT SQUASH)

Kids who don't eat meat will like these without the chicken. Or you can also puree the chicken after cooking and add to the bean mixture.

Prep: 15 minutes • Total: 25 minutes • Serves 4 • Packable

- **Nonstick cooking spray**
- **1 tablespoon olive oil**
- **½ pound chicken cutlets or boneless chicken breast, rinsed and dried**
- **½ teaspoon salt**
- **⅛ teaspoon pepper**
- **⅛ teaspoon chili powder, or to taste**
- **½ cup canned navy beans, drained and rinsed**
- **½ cup reduced-fat sour cream**
- **½ cup butternut squash puree**
- **½ cup shredded reduced-fat Cheddar cheese**
- **4 (8-inch) whole-wheat tortillas**
- **½ cup bottled salsa**

1 Preheat the oven to 400°F. Coat a large baking sheet with cooking spray.

2 Coat a large nonstick skillet with cooking spray and set it over medium-high heat. When the pan is hot, add the oil. Sprinkle the chicken with salt, pepper, and chili powder, add it to the pan, and cook until no longer pink in the center, 4 to 5 minutes per side for cutlets. For chicken breast, cook 5 minutes per side, reduce heat to low, cover, and cook 9 to 10 minutes longer. Cut the chicken into thin slices, or puree it, if necessary.

3 In a small bowl or mini-chopper, mash the beans with the sour cream. In another bowl, stir together the butternut squash puree and the cheese.

4 Spread the bean mixture over two of the tortillas, then arrange the chicken slices or spread the pureed chicken on top. Spread the cheese mixture over the other two tortillas and press one of each together to form sandwiches. Place on the baking sheet and bake until the tortillas are crisp, 5 to 6 minutes. Cut into wedges and serve with salsa.

Table Rules

IT'S BEEN important for me to set rules that I'm comfortable with and can uphold at the table. Some teach basic social skills, some teach good manners. These are my house rules (and you can decide which may work for you):

✔ No toys at the table. I have too many kids and each of them having a toy is too chaotic.

✔ No television or other forms of entertainment.

✔ If kids can't play, neither can adults. That means no phone calls, grown-ups!

✔ Everyone feeds him or herself—age appropriate.

✔ Children help set the table, clear plates, and take turns helping clean up the baby's mess. We keep a small dustpan and mini-sweeper in the kitchen.

✔ We don't talk with our mouths full, or walk around when eating—it's not safe!

✔ If a child is playing with her food and no longer eating, it means mealtime is over for her.

✔ Politeness is best taught by example. We're careful to say our pleases and thank yous and keep our elbows off the table so that the kids will follow our lead.

✔ Napkins on laps is advanced etiquette but I make a game of putting mine on my own lap with a grand flourish, and the kids want to do it, too!

Salsa Dip

(WITH RED PEPPER OR CARROT)

If you know that your kids like taco sauce, I'd recommend this dip in place of salsa. Serve with a bowl of raw veggies or baked tortilla chips. Or serve with tacos.

Total: 5 minutes • Serves 6

- **1 cup canned refried black or kidney beans**
- **1 cup bottled salsa**
- **4 ounces reduced-fat cream cheese, softened**
- **¼ cup red pepper or carrot puree**
- **1 tablespoon taco seasoning (without MSG)**

In a medium bowl, combine the beans, salsa, cream cheese, vegetable puree, and taco seasoning, and mash with a wooden spoon until combined. Serve at room temperature, or heat in the microwave for 1 minute.

Jerry: *My friends and I like to snack on this during the Super Bowl—and anything else.*

Creamy Potato Soup

(WITH CAULIFLOWER AND BUTTERNUT SQUASH OR CARROT)

I serve this when one of my kids has a tummy ache or the sniffles. It's soothing but nutritious.

Prep: 15 minutes • Total: 45 minutes • Serves 8 • No meat

- **Nonstick cooking spray**
- **2 teaspoons olive oil**
- **1 small onion, chopped**
- **1 clove garlic, cut in half**
- **2 (14-ounce) cans reduced-fat low-sodium chicken broth**
- **2 pounds potatoes, any kind, peeled and chopped**
- **½ cup cauliflower puree**
- **1½ cups butternut squash or carrot puree**
- **1 cup lowfat (1%) buttermilk**
- **½ teaspoon salt**
- **¼ cup shredded reduced-fat Cheddar cheese (optional)**
- **store-bought croutons (optional)**

1 Coat a large pot with cooking spray and set it over medium heat. When the pot is hot, add the oil, onion, and then the garlic, and cook, stirring occasionally, until the onion is soft but not brown, 5 to 6 minutes. (Be careful not to burn the garlic!)

2 Add the broth and potatoes and bring to a boil. Reduce the heat and simmer, partially covered, until the potatoes are tender, 20 to 25 minutes.

3 Carefully spoon the mixture into a blender or food processor and add the vegetable purees, buttermilk, and salt; puree until smooth. Ladle into bowls and sprinkle with cheese, if you like.

Julian: *This is soup? It tastes like mashed potatoes!*

Lasagna

(WITH SWEET POTATO AND CAULIFLOWER)

To speed things up, you can use a 24-ounce jar of your favorite tomato sauce in place of the canned tomatoes, onion, and garlic. Just stir the Parmesan into the sauce. And you can go meatless by leaving out the turkey or sirloin.

Prep: 20 minutes • Total: 70 minutes • Serves 8 to 10

- **Nonstick cooking spray**
- **1 tablespoon olive oil**
- **1 pound lean ground turkey or sirloin**
- **1 teaspoon salt**
- **¼ teaspoon pepper**
- **1 tablespoon all-purpose or whole-wheat flour**
- **3 cloves garlic, chopped**
- **2 tablespoons reduced-fat sour cream**
- **½ cup sweet potato puree**
- **½ cup grated Parmesan**
- **1 (26-ounce) or 2 (15-ounce) cans whole, peeled tomatoes, with their juice**
- **1 small onion, chopped**
- **1 cup lowfat (1%) cottage cheese**
- **1 large egg white**
- **½ cup cauliflower puree**
- **1 (8-ounce) box no-boil lasagna noodles**
- **2 cups shredded part-skim mozzarella**

1 Preheat the oven to 350°F. Coat an 8x12-inch baking dish with cooking spray.

2 For the meat filling, coat a large nonstick skillet with cooking spray and set it over medium-high heat. When the pan is hot, add the oil. Add the turkey or beef, sprinkle with salt and pepper, and cook, stirring occasionally, until the meat is no longer pink, 4 to 5 minutes. Sprinkle in the flour and half of the garlic, stir, and cook for 1 to 2 minutes longer. Off the heat, stir in the sour cream, sweet potato puree, and half (¼ cup) of the Parmesan; set aside.

3 For the sauce, combine the tomatoes and juice, the onion, and the remaining garlic and Parmesan (¼ cup) in a food processor or blender and process until smooth. Transfer the sauce to a bowl or large measuring cup. Or use jarred sauce and just add Parmesan.

4 In the same blender or food processor, blend the cottage cheese, egg white, and cauliflower puree until smooth; set aside.

5 To assemble the lasagna, spread 1 cup of the tomato sauce over the bottom of the baking dish. Layer about one-third of the noodles on top, covering the sauce completely. Spread the meat filling over them. (If you are going meatless, just add a first layer of cottage cheese.) Cover with another one-third of the noodles and then spread all of the cottage cheese mixture over them. Make another layer with the rest of the noodles and spoon the remaining tomato sauce over the top. Sprinkle evenly with mozzarella.

6 Cover the lasagna with aluminum foil and bake until the cheese has melted and the noodles are cooked through, about 40 minutes. Remove the foil and bake for 10 minutes longer, or until the top is bubbly and browned.

Jessica: *This is always a crowd-pleaser, and the no-boil noodles make it simple and easy to prepare.*

On the Job Training

I GIVE MY KIDS age-appropriate jobs to do around mealtimes, including setting and clearing the table and serving themselves. It's a more positive way to get them to the dinner table. They like being a part of mealtime, and they come to the table excited to be doing something productive and helpful. Serving themselves makes children feel independent and engaged—they feel that they're choosing what to eat rather than being forced to eat what they're served.

Speaking of jobs, I try to make it my kids' job to pack their own snacks. They love to:

1 Wash and dry fruit and vegetables.

2 Count things out and put them in plastic bags.

3 Fold napkins.

4 Then we put everything on the floor on a towel and they pack it up themselves as best they can.

Grilled Cheese Sandwiches

(WITH SWEET POTATO OR BUTTERNUT SQUASH)

It sure looks *like your average American grilled cheese.*

Prep: 5 minutes • Total: 15 minutes • Serves 2 • No meat

- **½ cup shredded reduced-fat Cheddar cheese**
- ½ cup sweet potato or butternut squash puree
- **1 tablespoon trans-fat-free soft tub margarine spread**
- **¼ teaspoon salt**
- **4 slices whole-wheat bread**
- **Nonstick cooking spray**
- **1 teaspoon olive oil**

1 In a medium bowl, mix the cheese, vegetable puree, margarine, and salt. Spread two slices of the bread with the cheese mixture and top with the other two slices.

2 Coat a large nonstick skillet with cooking spray and set it over medium heat. When the skillet is hot, add the oil. Put the sandwiches in the pan and spray the tops with cooking spray. Cook 4 to 5 minutes per side, until the bread is crisp and the filling is melted.

Jerry: Even I can make these.

Julian: Not as good as Mommy.

Avocado Spread

(WITH AVOCADO, OBVIOUSLY)

This is our version of guacamole, which, despite being light green, is somehow still popular at our house.

Prep and serve: 8 minutes • Makes 1½ cups

- 1 cup avocado puree
- ½ cup nonfat plain yogurt
- 1 tablespoon lowfat or reduced-fat mayonnaise
- 1 tablespoon lemon or lime juice
- ½ teaspoon salt
- ⅛ teaspoon garlic powder

In a medium bowl, stir together the avocado puree, yogurt, mayonnaise, lemon or lime juice, salt, and garlic powder with a fork or wooden spoon. If not serving immediately, lay a sheet of plastic wrap directly on the surface and press with your fingers to seal out the air. This will keep the vivid green color from darkening. Refrigerate in an airtight container for up to 2 days, or freeze for up to 1 month.

Julian: *I like this on my tacos!*

Sascha: *I don't.*

Jessica: *Shhh! She has it in her quesadillas!*

Twice-Baked Potatoes

(WITH CAULIFLOWER)

If you use a microwave, this is a "ready in 10 minutes" meal.
For a meatless version, just leave off the turkey bacon.

Prep: 15 minutes • Total: 80–85 minutes • Serves 4

- 4 large baking potatoes
- 1 cup cauliflower puree
- ½ cup reduced-fat sour cream
- 2 tablespoons trans-fat-free soft tub margarine spread
- 1 clove garlic, minced
- ¼ teaspoon salt
- ¼ teaspoon pepper
- 2 slices turkey bacon, cooked according to package directions and crumbled (optional)

1 Preheat the oven to 400°F.

2 Scrub the potatoes and prick them all over with a fork. Place them on a foil-lined baking sheet and bake until a knife penetrates easily, 50 to 55 minutes.

3 When the potatoes are cool enough to handle, cut them in half lengthwise and scoop out the pulp, leaving a thin (about ⅓ inch) shell.

4 Mash the potato pulp with the cauliflower puree, sour cream, margarine, garlic, salt, and pepper. Spoon the mixture back into the potato shells. Place the potatoes on the baking sheet and bake for 15 minutes. Sprinkle with bacon, if using.

Variation

Top with a sprinkling of shredded reduced-fat Cheddar or part-skim mozzarella, or a dollop of plain yogurt (preferably Greek) or lowfat cottage cheese before baking.

Waffle Sandwiches

(WITH SWEET POTATO)

These aren't really waffles, just whole-wheat bread slices toasted and crisped in a waffle maker. Your kids will love the "waffle" texture, and they'll never guess that there's sweet potato in the yummy filling.

Prep: 5 minutes • Total: 8 minutes • Serves 4 • No meat

- ½ cup nonfat or lowfat (1%) cottage cheese
- ½ cup sweet potato puree
- 1 large egg white
- 1 teaspoon firmly packed light or dark brown sugar
- ¼ teaspoon salt
- 8 slices whole-wheat bread, crusts removed

1 Preheat an electric waffle maker.

2 In a blender or food processor, blend the cottage cheese, sweet potato puree, egg white, brown sugar, and salt. Spread 4 slices of bread with the mixture and top with the remaining slices.

3 Place the sandwiches two at a time in the waffle maker and close the lid. Cook for 2 to 3 minutes, until the sandwiches hold together and the filling is no longer runny.

Variation

Thaw frozen whole-grain waffles, and sandwich the filling between two of them. Coat a nonstick skillet with cooking spray and set it over medium heat. When the pan is hot, add 1 teaspoon vegetable oil, then the "wafflewiches," and cook for 4 to 5 minutes on each side on until the filling is cooked.

Social Creatures

I'VE LEARNED food goes down better in a social environment that brings the family together. A warm family atmosphere gives a child something to do other than stare at his plate, and a picky child who eats alone is likely to be pickier because there is little distraction. I try to duplicate the happy mealtimes of my own childhood, which were sociable and relaxed, with easygoing conversation. (Oh, wait a minute, that was a dream I had!)

Seriously, though, the moment I put the food down on the table, I sweep the children up in a lively conversation about my day. They answer with their own stories, and before you know it, mealtime is over, without a hiccup! Realistically, in this day and age, it's very difficult for many families to actually sit down together. Even if you can't be there with your children, ask whoever is taking care of them to sit with them—even if he or she is not eating—and make conversation.

Pink Pancakes

(WITH BEET)

Take a store-bought pancake mix, fortify it with grated apple, a little beet puree, and some ricotta cheese—it's a full-protein meal.

Prep: 10 minutes • Total: 13–15 minutes • Serves 4 little children

- ¾ cup water
- ½ cup ricotta cheese
- ¼ cup beet puree
- 1 teaspoon pure vanilla extract
- ½ teaspoon cinnamon
- 1 cup pancake mix
- ¼ cup grated apple
- Nonstick cooking spray
- 1 tablespoon canola or vegetable oil
- Pure maple syrup or fruit, for serving

1 In a blender or food processor, combine the water, ricotta cheese, beet puree, vanilla, and cinnamon and blend. Dump the mixture into a medium bowl, add the pancake mix and apple, and stir until just combined. Do not overmix—the batter will be a little lumpy.

2 Coat a griddle or large nonstick skillet with cooking spray and set it over medium-high heat. When hot, add the oil. Spoon the batter onto the griddle or skillet, using about ¼ cup batter for each pancake. Cook the pancakes until bubbles form on top and the batter is set, 1 to 2 minutes. Then flip the pancakes with a spatula and cook until golden brown on the other side, 2 to 3 minutes. Serve warm, with syrup or fruit.

Julian: Pancakes for dinner? I think my mom is crazy sometimes!

Tortilla "Cigars"

(WITH YELLOW SQUASH AND CARROT)

These are very popular at our house. They pack well for picnics or lunches on the go because they can also be served cold. For a vegetarian meal, leave out the chicken or turkey.

Prep: 10 minutes • Total: 15 minutes • Serves 6 • Packable

- **1 cup sautéed or roasted chicken or turkey, cubed (or pureed)**
- **½ cup shredded reduced-fat Cheddar or American cheese**
- **½ cup yellow squash puree**
- **½ cup carrot puree**
- **4 ounces reduced-fat or nonfat cream cheese**
- **¼ teaspoon garlic powder**
- **¼ teaspoon salt**
- **6 large (burrito-size) whole-wheat tortillas**

1 Preheat the oven to 350°F. Line baking sheets with aluminum foil or parchment paper.

2 In a large bowl, stir together the chicken or turkey, cheese, squash and carrot purees, cream cheese, garlic powder, and salt.

3 Cut the tortillas in half. Place one half on the work surface with the straight edge facing you. Spread about two tablespoons of the filling along that edge from one side to the other. Starting at the edge, roll the tortilla into a cigar shape, completely enclosing the filling. Place seam-side down on the baking sheet. Stuff and roll the rest of the tortillas the same way.

4 Bake until the tortillas begin to brown, 4 to 5 minutes. Let cool slightly before serving.

Shepherd: *Mmmm . . . good!*

Sloppy Joes

(WITH SWEET POTATO AND BUTTERNUT SQUASH OR RED PEPPER)

I serve this in hotdog buns. A hotdog bun filled with something that's not a hotdog is very funny to some kids!

Prep: 25 minutes • Total: 45 minutes • Serves 8

- **Nonstick cooking spray**
- **1 tablespoon olive oil**
- **½ cup chopped red onion**
- **½ cup chopped celery**
- **2 cloves garlic, minced**
- **1 pound lean ground turkey or sirloin**
- **½ cup sweet potato puree**
- **½ cup butternut squash or red pepper puree**
- **raw, finely chopped carrots (optional)**
- **½ cup reduced-fat low-sodium beef broth**
- **¼ cup tomato paste**
- **1 tablespoon Worcestershire sauce**
- **1 teaspoon chili powder, or to taste**
- **½ teaspoon salt**
- **⅛ teaspoon pepper**
- **8 whole-grain hamburger or hot-dog buns**

1 Coat a large nonstick skillet with cooking spray and set it over medium-high heat. When the skillet is hot, add the oil. Add the onion, celery, and garlic, and cook until the onion starts to soften (not brown), 3 to 4 minutes.

2 Add the meat, breaking it up with a wooden spoon, and cook until no longer pink, 4 to 5 minutes.

3 Add the vegetable purees, raw chopped carrot (if using) beef broth, tomato paste, Worcestershire sauce, chili powder, salt, and pepper. Reduce the heat to low, cover, and simmer until the liquid is reduced by about one-half, 15 to 20 minutes.

4 Spoon the mixture over buns and serve.

Shepherd: *Hot dog?*

Sascha: *No, silly! It's Mommy's Sloppy Joes.*

Tacos

(WITH SWEET POTATO OR CARROT OR BUTTERNUT SQUASH)

Cooking the meat in crushed tomatoes and adding a puree means this meal is loaded with nutrients. It's fun for kids to choose their own toppings and stuff the tacos themselves.

Prep: 10 minutes • Total: 30 minutes • Serves 6 to 8

- **Nonstick cooking spray**
- **1 tablespoon olive oil**
- **1 pound lean ground sirloin or turkey**
- **1 (14-ounce) can crushed tomatoes, with their juice**
- **½ cup sweet potato, carrot, or butternut squash puree**
- **½ (1.25-ounce) packet taco seasoning, with no MSG**
- **1 package taco shells (18 shells)**
- **½ cup shredded reduced-fat mozzarella or Cheddar cheese**

TOPPINGS
- **½ pound cherry tomatoes, stemmed and quartered**
- **½ cup canned or frozen corn kernels**
- **¼ cup lowfat sour cream**
- **3 large leaves Romaine lettuce, thinly sliced crosswise**
- **½ small avocado, pitted, peeled, and sliced**
- **1 small red pepper, stemmed, seeded, and finely sliced**

1 Coat a large nonstick skillet with cooking spray and set it over medium-high heat. When the skillet is hot, add the oil. Add the meat, breaking it up with a spoon. Brown for 4 to 5 minutes, stirring occasionally.

2 Stir in the tomatoes and their juice, vegetable puree, and seasoning mix. Reduce the heat to low and simmer until the meat is no longer pink and the mixture begins to thicken, 10 to 15 minutes longer.

3 Preheat the oven to 325°F. Fill the taco shells with the meat mixture and sprinkle with cheese. Stand the shells in a baking dish and bake until the cheese melts, 5 to 10 minutes. Add your favorite toppings.

Turkey Chili

(WITH RED PEPPER AND CARROT)

If your children freak out when they see beans, puree them before adding them to the chili. You can also finely chop raw carrot and pepper in the food processor to save time.

Prep: 15 minutes • Total: 35 minutes • Serves 8

- Nonstick cooking spray
- 1 tablespoon olive oil
- ½ cup chopped red onion
- 1 pound ground lean turkey
- 2 cloves garlic, minced
- 1 tablespoon chili powder, or to taste
- 1 teaspoon salt
- ¼ teaspoon sweet paprika
- ⅛ teaspoon pepper
- 1 (15-ounce) can chopped tomatoes
- 1 (26-ounce) carton reduced-fat low-sodium chicken broth
- ½ cup red pepper puree
- ½ cup carrot puree
- ¼ cup cornmeal
- 2 tablespoons flaxseed meal
- 1 (15-ounce) can kidney beans, drained and rinsed

1 Coat the bottom of a large pot with cooking spray and set it over medium heat. When the pot is hot, add the oil. Add the onion and cook until it begins to soften, about 2 minutes.

2 Meanwhile, sprinkle the turkey with the garlic, chili powder, salt, paprika, and pepper. Add the turkey to the pot and cook, stirring occasionally, until the turkey is no longer pink, 5 to 6 minutes.

3 Stir in the tomatoes. Add the broth, red pepper puree, carrot puree, cornmeal, and flaxseed meal, and stir well. Bring to a boil, reduce the heat, and simmer, covered, 15 to 20 minutes, or until the flavors have blended. Stir in the beans and cook a little longer, just to heat them through.

Sascha: *Ew, beans are gross.*

Jessica: *Next time I'll puree them.*

Couscous

(WITH YELLOW SQUASH AND CARROT)

Yellow squash is the same color as the couscous . . .

Prep: 6 minutes • Total: 13 minutes • Serves 8 • Packable

- ½ cup reduced-fat low-sodium chicken broth
- 1 cup regular or whole-wheat couscous
- ½ cup yellow squash puree
- ¼ cup carrot puree
- 2 tablespoons trans-fat-free soft tub margarine spread
- 1 tablespoon grated Parmesan
- 1 clove garlic, minced (optional)
- ½ teaspoon salt
- ¼ teaspoon pepper

1 Bring the broth to a boil in a medium saucepan.

2 Turn off the heat, stir in the couscous, squash puree, carrot puree, margarine, Parmesan, garlic, salt, and pepper. Cover and let stand for 6 to 7 minutes, until all the liquid is absorbed and the couscous is soft.

Joy: This is a super low-calorie side dish (only 40 calories and less than 1 gram total fat per ½-cup serving) thanks to the vegetable purees—each adds volume, lowering the overall calories in an otherwise typically starchy side dish. Carrots add beta carotene—good for kids' eyes!

Mealtime Tips

As a mother who is concerned and curious about the issues surrounding food and children, I have had lengthy conversations with Patricia Schimm and Jean Mandelbaum, my parenting "gurus." They explained to me that the more pressure and control we try to exert on our children, the more we are setting ourselves up not only for an unpleasant mealtime, but for our children having potential food issues later on. In fact, both experts agree that kids will eat almost anything if there is no power struggle involved. Pat Schimm even goes so far as to say that if you talk about topics *other* than food at the table, you are likely to have better results. These are more tips and advice I have learned from Pat and Jean:

1 As a general rule, don't force children to eat—they won't starve.

2 Typical toddlers will be challenging, picky, and even difficult. That's normal—saying "no" to everything is their way of testing the limits of their safety in the world. At this age, handing them a plate of food will often result in "No, I don't like that." However, giving them the option of choosing among a few healthful foods—where no choice will be "wrong" or bad for them—is an optimal scenario for both parent and child.

3 When a child is old enough to feed him or herself—typically between 9- and 12-months old—parents should step back and allow them to take over. By feeding themselves, kids learn independence and self-reliance. A young child who can feed herself independently will likely turn out to be a good eater because she is doing it on her own, without anyone stepping on her territory. And, I make it easy for my kids to feed themselves because I don't make anything fussy or fancy.

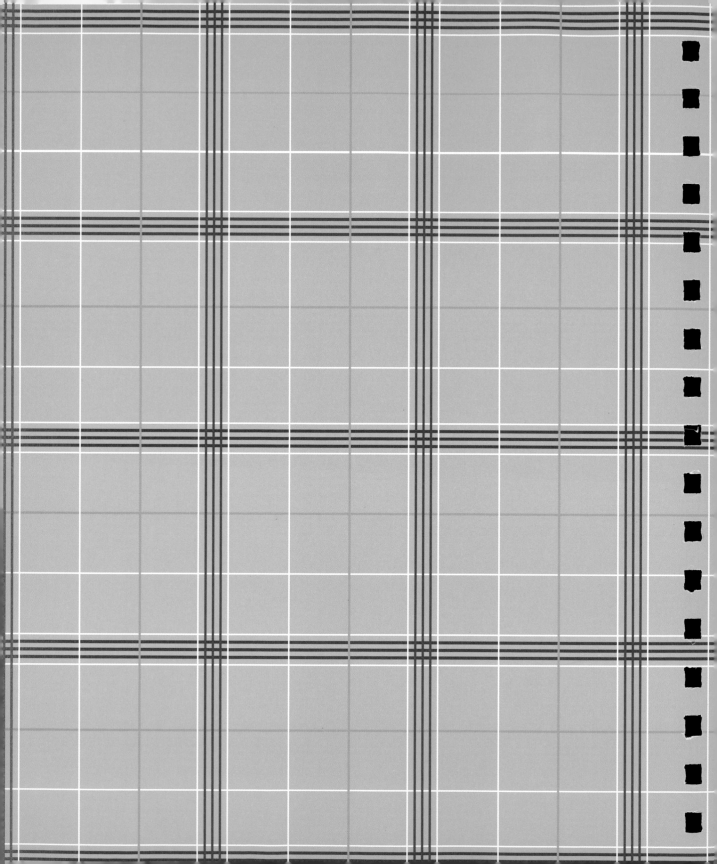

DESSERT

Brownies *156*

Chocolate Pudding *159*

Doughnuts *160*

Chocolate Peanut Butter Dip . *163*

Banana Marshmallow Dip *163*

Chocolate Chip Cupcakes *164*

Frozen Yogurt Pops *167*

Gingerbread Spice Cake *168*

Blueberry Oatmeal Bars *171*

Chocolate Cupcakes *172*

Chocolate Fondue *174*

Chocolate Chip Cookies *177*

Blueberry Cheesecake Cupcakes . *178*

Lemon Raspberry Cupcakes . . . *181*

Graham Cracker Ice Cream

   Sandwiches *182*

Carrot Cake Muffins *185*

Yellow Cake *186*

Hot Cocoa *189*

Fruit Punch *189*

Marshmallow Crispy Treats . . . *190*

Angel Food Cupcakes *193*

Chocolate Cake *194*

Oatmeal Raisin Cookies *197*

Chocolate Chip Muffins *198*

Banana Pudding Pie *201*

Brownies

(WITH CARROT AND SPINACH)

These brownies fool everyone! You won't believe how scrumptious they are (or how good they are for you) until you make them yourself. Just don't serve them warm—it's not until they're completely cool that the spinach flavor totally disappears.

Prep: 15 minutes • Total: 55 minutes • Makes 12 brownies • Packable

- **Nonstick cooking spray**
- **3 ounces semisweet or bittersweet chocolate**
- **½ cup carrot puree**
- **½ cup spinach puree**
- **½ cup firmly packed light or dark brown sugar**
- **¼ cup unsweetened cocoa powder**
- **2 tablespoons trans-fat-free soft tub margarine spread**
- **2 teaspoons pure vanilla extract**
- **2 large egg whites**
- **¾ cup oat flour, or all-purpose flour**
- **½ teaspoon baking powder**
- **½ teaspoon salt**

1 Preheat the oven to 350°F. Coat an 8x8-inch baking pan with cooking spray.

2 Melt the chocolate in a double boiler or over a very low flame.

3 In a large bowl, combine the melted chocolate, vegetable purees, sugar, cocoa powder, margarine, and vanilla, and whisk until smooth and creamy, 1 to 2 minutes.

4 Whisk in egg whites. Stir in the flour, baking powder, and salt with a wooden spoon.

5 Pour the batter into the pan and bake 35 to 40 minutes. Cool completely in the pan before cutting into 12 bars.

Joy: *These brownies are low in calories (only 133 per brownie) and saturated fat. They're also packed with 3 grams of fiber (which is just crazy for a brownie!), while spinach and carrots provide two powerful antioxidants that help your kids' eyes stay healthy.*

156

Chocolate Pudding

(WITH AVOCADO)

I love this pudding. Sometimes I don't want to share.

Prep: 5 minutes • Total: 9 minutes • Serves 8 to 10

- ¼ cup trans-fat-free soft tub margarine spread
- 1 cup avocado puree
- **1 cup confectioners' sugar**
- **½ cup unsweetened cocoa powder**
- **1 teaspoon pure vanilla extract**
- **¼ cup cornstarch**

In a medium saucepan, melt the margarine over low heat. Stir in the avocado puree, sugar, cocoa powder, and vanilla. Cook, mashing well with a silicone spatula to smooth out any lumps of avocado, until the mixture thickens, 3 to 4 minutes. Off the heat, gradually stir in the cornstarch. Serve warm.

Sascha: *Hey . . . where did Mom put the pudding?*

Doughnuts

(WITH PUMPKIN AND SWEET POTATO)

These are light and airy, and a little shake of powdered sugar makes them utterly irresistible.

Prep: 10 minutes • Total: 35 minutes • Makes 2 dozen mini-doughnuts

- **Nonstick cooking spray**
- **½ cup firmly packed light or dark brown sugar**
- **½ cup canned pumpkin puree**
- **½ cup sweet potato puree**
- **½ cup nonfat (skim) milk, or lowfat (1%) buttermilk**
- **1 large egg white**
- **1 tablespoon trans-fat-free soft tub margarine spread, melted**
- **1 teaspoon pure vanilla extract**
- **1 cup all-purpose flour, or whole-wheat pastry flour**
- **1 teaspoon baking soda**
- **½ teaspoon baking powder**
- **½ teaspoon cinnamon or pumpkin pie spice**
- **¼ cup confectioners' sugar**

1 Preheat the oven to 350°F. Coat a doughnut mold or 12-cup mini-muffin tin with cooking spray.

2 In a large bowl, beat together the sugar, pumpkin and sweet potato purees, milk, egg white, margarine, and vanilla. Add the flour, baking soda, baking powder, and spice, and mix until completely incorporated.

3 Pour the batter into a gallon-sized plastic bag (or pastry bag if you have one!) and cut the bottom tip off of one side of the bag. Squeeze the batter through, into the doughnut mold. Bake until the tops are lightly browned and a toothpick comes out clean when inserted, 20 to 25 minutes. Turn the doughnuts out onto a rack to cool. When cool, dust with confectioners' sugar.

4 Store in an airtight container at room temperature for up to 2 days, or freeze for up to 1 month.

Julian: My friends love my mom because she makes us doughnuts.

Chocolate Peanut Butter Dip

(WITH CARROT)

Serve as a snack or dessert with vegetable sticks or fresh fruit wedges.

Prep and serve: 5 minutes • Serves 4

- ½ cup (creamy) natural peanut butter
- ½ cup fat-free cream cheese
- 6 tablespoons chocolate syrup
- ¼ cup carrot puree
- ½ teaspoon salt
- fruit slices, for dipping

Stir the peanut butter, cream cheese, chocolate syrup, carrot puree, and salt together in a bowl until smooth.

Banana Marshmallow Dip

(WITH BUTTERNUT SQUASH)

Another veggie-filled dessert!

Prep and serve: 5 minutes • Serves 4

- 1 cup butternut squash puree
- 1 cup banana puree
- 1 cup mini-marshmallows
- Fruit slices, for dipping

In a microwavable bowl, stir together the squash and banana purees. Cover and microwave until warm, 1 to 2 minutes. Stir in the marshmallows and serve warm.

Chocolate Chip Cupcakes

(WITH PUMPKIN AND YELLOW SQUASH)

Chocolate chips and maple syrup, and the whole family is in heaven.

Prep: 10 minutes • Total: 35 minutes • Makes 12 cupcakes • Packable

CUPCAKE BATTER

- **Nonstick cooking spray**
- 1 cup canned pumpkin puree
- ½ cup yellow squash puree
- **½ cup firmly packed light or dark brown sugar**
- **½ cup water**
- **⅓ cup canola oil**
- **1 teaspoon pure vanilla extract**
- **2¼ cups all-purpose flour**
- **1½ teaspoons baking soda**
- **½ teaspoon salt**
- **½ cup semisweet chocolate chips**

FROSTING

- **1 (8-ounce) package reduced-fat cream cheese**
- **⅓ cup pure maple syrup**
- **2 teaspoons pure vanilla extract**
- **⅛ teaspoon salt**

1 Preheat the oven to 350°F. Coat a 12-cup muffin tin with cooking spray or line with paper baking cups.

2 Put the pumpkin and squash purees in a large mixing bowl or the bowl of an electric mixer. Add the brown sugar, water, oil, and vanilla, and beat until well blended.

3 Now add the flour, baking soda, salt, and chocolate chips, and mix until completely incorporated. Divide the batter among the muffin cups. Bake until the tops of the cupcakes are lightly browned and spring back to the touch, 20 to 25 minutes. Turn the cupcakes out onto a rack to cool before frosting them.

4 For the frosting, beat the cream cheese with the maple syrup, vanilla, and salt until smooth. Spread the frosting over the cooled cupcakes.

5 Store the cupcakes in an airtight container at room temperature for up to 2 days, or wrap individually and freeze for up to 1 month.

If We Whine, So Will They

ONE NIGHT, back when I used to beg my children to eat their vegetables, I heard myself groveling and pleading and realized that I was sounding just like them. It wasn't pretty. Everyone knows that children mimic their parents. I realized that if I whined at them about their vegetables, they'd whine back about that (and everything else).

Frozen Yogurt Pops
(WITH BERRIES)

Your kids think they're just getting a treat, but these popsicles are a great low-calorie, lowfat alternative to high-fat ice cream. If you're using raspberries, use ³/₄ cup sugar, because raspberries are tart.

Prep: 10 minutes • Freeze: 120 minutes • Makes 8 popsicles

- **2 cups plain lowfat yogurt**
- **2 cups frozen berries (strawberries, raspberries, blueberries, or cherries), thawed in the microwave for 1 minute**
- **¹/₂ to ³/₄ cup confectioners' sugar**

Combine the yogurt, fruit, and sugar in a blender or food processor and process until smooth. Pour into popsicle molds and freeze.

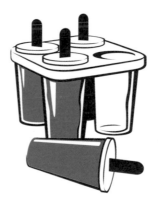

Joy: Each popsicle (only 100 calories!) contains less than 1 gram of fat. Calcium-rich yogurt helps build strong bones and teeth, and berries add a little vitamin C—an antioxidant that helps boost the immune system and aids in healing.

Gingerbread Spice Cake

(WITH BROCCOLI AND CARROT)

My kids would never eat this if they knew what was in it. Since they don't, it's usually gone in a day—or less.

Prep: 15 minutes • Total: 60 minutes • Serves 8 to 10 • Packable

- Nonstick cooking spray
- 1 cup whole-wheat flour
- 1 cup all-purpose flour
- 1 teaspoon baking soda
- 1 teaspoon ground ginger
- 1 teaspoon cinnamon
- ¼ teaspoon ground cloves
- ¼ teaspoon allspice
- ¼ teaspoon salt
- ¾ cup firmly packed light or dark brown sugar
- ¼ cup canola or vegetable oil
- 1 large egg
- 1 cup broccoli puree
- ½ cup carrot puree
- ½ cup nonfat plain yogurt
- ¼ cup molasses
- 2 teaspoons pure vanilla extract
- 1 tablespoon grated orange zest

1 Preheat the oven to 375°F. Coat a 9x5-inch loaf pan with cooking spray.

2 In a bowl or zipper-lock bag, mix the flours with the baking soda, ginger, cinnamon, cloves, allspice, and salt; set aside.

3 In a large mixing bowl or the bowl of an electric mixer, beat the sugar, oil, and egg until smooth. Beat in the vegetable purees, yogurt, molasses, vanilla, and orange zest. Add the flour mixture and mix until smooth.

4 Pour the batter into the pan and smooth the top. Bake until a toothpick comes out clean when inserted into the center of the cake, 45 to 50 minutes. Cool 5 minutes in the pan before turning the cake out onto a rack to cool completely.

Jerry: Powdered sugar makes me nutty.

Blueberry Oatmeal Bars
(WITH SPINACH)

Crunchy and sweet, but full of spinach! Let the bars cool completely before serving so that the taste of the spinach has a chance to disappear completely.

Prep: 10 minutes • Total: 50 minutes • Makes 12 bars

- **Nonstick cooking spray**
- **2 cups old-fashioned oats**
- **1¼ cups all-purpose flour**
- **½ cup sugar**
- **½ teaspoon cinnamon**
- **¼ teaspoon baking powder**
- **¼ teaspoon salt**
- **1 teaspoon pure vanilla extract**
- **¾ cup Balance trans-fat-free soft tub margarine spread, chilled**
- **1 cup low-sugar blueberry preserves**
- **½ cup spinach puree**

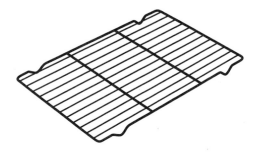

1 Preheat the oven to 375°F. Coat an 8x8-inch baking pan with cooking spray.

2 In a large bowl, combine the oats, flour, sugar, cinnamon, baking powder, salt, and vanilla, and stir to mix well.

3 Add the margarine and cut it quickly into the dry ingredients with two knives until the mixture resembles coarse meal and is no longer powdery. Do not overmix—bits of margarine will still be visible.

4 Set aside about half of the oat mixture; press the rest of it firmly into the pan. Bake until lightly browned at the edges (but not fully baked), 13 to 15 minutes.

5 Meanwhile, mix the preserves with the spinach puree in a small bowl.

6 Spread the blueberry mixture over the partially baked oat layer, then sprinkle with the reserved oat mixture. Bake until the topping is slightly browned, 20 to 25 minutes. Set the pan on a rack to cool completely before cutting into 12 bars.

Chocolate Cupcakes

(WITH AVOCADO AND CAULIFLOWER)

These are a favorite of my son Julian. I brought them to class to celebrate his fourth birthday, and his classmates went through them in seconds. The taste of the avocado is still slightly detectable when the cupcakes are warm, so be sure they're completely cool before you serve them.

Prep: 15 minutes • Total: 35 minutes • Makes 12 cupcakes • Packable

CUPCAKE BATTER
- **Nonstick cooking spray**
- **1 cup avocado puree**
- **1½ cups sugar**
- **1 cup nonfat (skim) milk**
- **2 teaspoons pure vanilla extract**
- **½ teaspoon balsamic vinegar**
- **2 large egg whites**
- **2 cups all-purpose flour**
- **½ cup unsweetened cocoa powder**
- **1 teaspoon baking soda**
- **½ teaspoon salt**

FROSTING
- **1 (8-ounce) package reduced-fat cream cheese**
- **½ cup confectioners' sugar**
- **¼ cup cauliflower puree**
- **2 tablespoons pure vanilla extract**
- **⅛ teaspoon salt**

1 Preheat the oven to 350°F. Coat a 12-cup muffin tin with cooking spray or line with paper baking cups.

2 In a large mixing bowl or the bowl of an electric mixer, beat the avocado puree, sugar, milk, vanilla, and vinegar until smooth. Beat in the egg whites one at a time, just until incorporated.

3 Add the flour, cocoa powder, baking soda, and salt, and mix until smooth. Divide the batter among the muffin cups. Bake until the tops of the cupcakes are lightly browned and spring back to the touch, 15 to 20 minutes. Turn out onto a rack to cool completely before frosting them.

4 For the frosting, beat together the cream cheese, sugar, cauliflower puree, vanilla, and salt until smooth. Spread over the cooled cupcakes.

5 Store the cupcakes in an airtight container at room temperature for up to 2 days, or freeze for up to 1 month.

(OTHER) MOTHERS KNOW BEST

(PART 3)

"Marketing is everything when talking to kids about vegetables! Broccoli with marinara sauce to dip it in is billed as 'Shrek's trees with swamp mud.' Asparagus served with a side of melted butter becomes 'princess wands with magic sauce.' The fast-food companies and sugar cereals do it so well—we parents have to make veggies sassy, too."

— Elizabeth, Los Angeles
MOTHER OF ISABEL, 8, AND CAROLINE, 6

"We mix cold-pressed flaxseed oil in oatmeal and all kinds of purees. We sprinkle flaxseed meal on yogurt, on cereal, on anything crunchy. We also make cookies with barley flour and sweetened with maple syrup—anything to get whole grains in there. When the kids were babies, we started pureeing brown rice, so they have always had a taste for it. We make tofu chocolate pie, which they love. We also make veggie chili with a dollop of yogurt on top instead of sour cream and put organic corn chips on the side for dipping."

—The Martin Family, New York City
CHILDREN AGES 3 AND 1

"When Alex is resistant to vegetables or other healthy foods, I resort to saying, 'Please just take X more bites!' (Sometimes X is 7, sometimes it's 4, for example). Sometimes I sprinkle powdered cheddar cheese on certain vegetables. If I'm really desperate, we do a 'strawberry dance' (the name of the dance changes depending on the name of the food), a funny dance before taking each bite of the food. Pathetic, I know."

—Elzy, Burlington, Vermont
MOTHER OF ALEX, 3, AND DANIEL, 1

Chocolate Fondue

(WITH AVOCADO AND CARROT)

Children love to dip. Try lowfat graham crackers, apple slices, strawberries—so good!

Prep and serve: 5 minutes • Serves 4

- **1 tablespoon trans-fat-free soft tub margarine spread**
- **½ cup avocado puree**
- **¼ cup carrot puree**
- **1 cup confectioners' sugar**
- **½ cup unsweetened cocoa powder**
- **1 teaspoon pure vanilla extract**
- **Sliced fruits, whole berries, or cherries, for dipping**

Melt the margarine over low heat in a medium saucepan. Add the avocado and carrot purees, sugar, cocoa powder, and vanilla, and whisk well until smooth. Serve warm, with fruit.

Julian: *I make a chocolate sandwich with graham crackers.*

Sascha: *Hey . . . don't copy me!*

Chocolate Chip Cookies

(WITH CHICKPEAS)

These are so easy and fast to make, but watch out for flying chickpeas! If using a standing mixer, partially cover the bowl with a dish towel to keep the chickpeas from flying out. (Of course my kids think it's hysterical when this happens.)

Prep: 20 minutes • Total: 31-33 minutes • Makes 2 dozen cookies • Packable

- **Nonstick cooking spray**
- **1 cup firmly packed light or dark brown sugar**
- **¾ cup trans-fat-free soft tub margarine spread**
- **2 large egg whites**
- **2 teaspoons pure vanilla extract**
- 1 (15-ounce) can chickpeas, drained and rinsed
- **2 cups (12 ounces) semisweet chocolate chips**
- **¾ cup chopped walnuts (optional)**
- **¾ cup raisins (optional)**
- **2 cups all-purpose flour**
- **½ cup old-fashioned oats**
- **1 teaspoon baking soda**
- **¼ teaspoon salt**

1 Preheat the oven to 350°F. Coat a baking sheet with cooking spray.

2 In a large mixing bowl or the bowl of an electric mixer, beat the sugar and margarine with a wooden spoon or on medium speed until smooth. Beat in the egg whites and vanilla, then the chickpeas and chocolate chips. Add the flour, oats, baking soda, and salt, and mix on low speed until a thick dough forms.

3 Drop the dough by the tablespoonful onto the baking sheet, spacing the cookies about 2 inches apart. Press gently with a fork to flatten. Bake until the cookies are golden brown and just set, 11 to 13 minutes; do not overbake. Transfer to a rack to cool.

4 Store in an airtight container for up to 3 days.

Blueberry Cheesecake Cupcakes

(WITH YELLOW SQUASH, BLUEBERRY, AND SPINACH)

Kids love the sweet cream surprise in the center of these Blueberry cupcakes.

Prep: 10 minutes • Total: 35 minutes • Makes 12 cupcakes • Packable

- **Nonstick cooking spray**

FILLING
- **4 ounces reduced-fat or nonfat cream cheese**
- **⅓ cup confectioners' sugar**
- **½ cup yellow squash puree**
- **1 large egg white**
- **⅛ teaspoon salt**

CUPCAKE BATTER
- **1 cup granulated sugar**
- **½ cup nonfat (skim) milk**
- **½ cup blueberry puree**
- **½ cup spinach puree**
- **¼ cup canola or vegetable oil**
- **1 cup all-purpose flour**
- **1½ teaspoons baking soda**
- **¼ teaspoon salt**

1 Preheat the oven to 350°F. Coat a 12-cup muffin tin with cooking spray or line with paper baking cups.

2 For the filling, beat the cream cheese, sugar, squash puree, egg white, and salt in a bowl until smooth; set aside.

3 For the batter, combine the sugar, milk, blueberry and spinach purees, and oil in a large bowl or the bowl of an electric mixer and beat until smooth. Add flour, baking soda, and salt, and mix until just combined.

4 Using about half the total amount of batter, fill each muffin cup about one-third full. Drop a tablespoonful of the filling on top of each, and cover with the rest of the batter. Bake until the tops of the cupcakes are lightly browned and spring back to the touch, 20 to 25 minutes. Turn the cupcakes out onto a rack to cool.

5 Store in an airtight container at room temperature for up to 2 days, or wrap individually and freeze for up to 1 month.

More Mealtime Tips

1. Eating about a fistful of food is a typical meal for a hungry toddler. Toddlers are busy and active and for many, sitting at the table eating is an activity that is difficult to sustain after they have eased their hunger.

2. Giving children heaping platefuls of food is overwhelming for them. You can let them feel a sense of accomplishment by finishing small portions and then asking for "more, please!" At my house, I give them tiny portions and I watch as their eyes light up with excitement as they refill their own plates.

3. Bribing with sweets is not a good solution for handling misbehavior. Using sweets as a reward inflates their value and encourages children to associate sweets with emotional fulfillment.

4. Try to moderate junk food intake. On the other hand, avoid extremes as well. What is forbidden sometimes holds a special attraction for children. If you offer healthful treats toward the end of mealtime, such as my chocolate chip or oatmeal raisin cookies, you will find your children start to lose interest in what they do not have.

5. Parents who have good eating and exercise habits will provide their children with the best possible foundation for overall healthy habits. The best way to raise children with healthy habits is to set a good example.

Lemon Raspberry Cupcakes

(WITH YELLOW SQUASH AND BEETS)

This recipe works just as well as a cake. Bake 40 to 45 minutes in a 9-inch cake pan. Let cool 5 minutes in the pan before turning the cake out onto a rack to cool.

Prep: 15 minutes • Total: 40 minutes • Makes 12 cupcakes or a 9-inch cake

- **Nonstick cooking spray**

FILLING
- **¼ cup frozen raspberries, thawed**
- **2 tablespoons beet puree**
- **2 tablespoons confectioners' sugar**
- **1 tablespoon trans-fat-free soft tub margarine spread**

BATTER
- **1 cup granulated sugar**
- **½ cup nonfat (skim) milk**
- **½ cup yellow squash puree**
- **⅓ cup canola or vegetable oil**
- **2 large egg whites**
- **2 tablespoons lemon juice**
- **1 teaspoon pure lemon extract**
- **2 cups all-purpose flour**
- **2 teaspoons baking powder**
- **¼ teaspoon salt**

FROSTING (OPTIONAL)
- **1 (8-ounce) package reduced-fat cream cheese**
- **½ cup confectioners' sugar**
- **1 teaspoon pure lemon extract**

1 Preheat the oven to 350°F. Coat a 12-cup muffin tin with cooking spray or line with paper baking cups.

2 For the filling, puree the raspberries, beet puree, sugar, and margarine in a blender or food processor; set aside.

3 For the batter, beat the sugar in a large bowl with the milk, yellow squash puree, oil, egg whites, lemon juice, and lemon extract until smooth. Add the flour, baking powder, and salt, then mix until incorporated.

4 Using about half the batter, fill each muffin cup one-third full. Dot each with the raspberry filling, then cover with the rest of the batter.

5 Bake until the tops of the cupcakes are lightly browned and spring back to the touch, 20 to 25 minutes. Turn the cupcakes out onto a rack to cool.

6 For the frosting, beat together the cream cheese, sugar, and lemon extract. Spread the frosting over the cooled cupcakes.

Graham Cracker Ice Cream Sandwiches

My children practically cheer when I bring these out. I wrap them in waxed paper so the kids have fun opening them (and because they keep better in the freezer). Dip the edges of the sandwiches in coconut for an adorable presentation.

Prep: 5 minutes • Total: 120 minutes • Makes 8 sandwiches

- **2 cups lowfat plain yogurt**
- **1 cup sugar**
- **1 cup lowfat (1%) buttermilk**
- **2 tablespoons lemon juice**
- **Grated zest of 1 lemon**
- **16 lowfat graham crackers, broken in half (32 squares)**
- **Shredded coconut (optional)**

1 In a large bowl, whisk together the yogurt, sugar, buttermilk, lemon juice, and lemon zest. Transfer to a small bowl, cover, and freeze for 1 to 1½ hours, until the mixture starts to thicken.

2 To form the sandwiches, scoop out and then press about ¼ cup of the semifrozen yogurt mixture between two graham cracker squares. Wrap each in waxed paper and freeze 30 minutes, or until firm.

3 If using coconut, put some on a plate and dip all four edges of the sandwich to coat.

Jerry: *I'm going to request these at my last meal.*

Carrot Cake Muffins

(WITH CARROT AND CAULIFLOWER)

My friends are always begging me to make these. And when I do, none of us want to share them with our children!

Prep: 10 minutes • Total: 35 minutes • Makes 12 muffins • Packable

- Nonstick cooking spray
- ½ cup firmly packed light or dark brown sugar
- 4 tablespoons trans-fat-free soft tub margarine spread
- 1 cup carrot puree
- ½ cup cauliflower puree
- 1 large egg
- 2 tablespoons frozen orange juice concentrate
- 1 teaspoon pure vanilla extract
- ¼ cup dried apricots, chopped
- ¼ cup pitted prunes, chopped
- 2 cups all-purpose flour
- 1 teaspoon baking powder
- 1 teaspoon baking soda
- 1 teaspoon cinnamon
- ¼ teaspoon allspice

FROSTING (OPTIONAL)
- 1 (8-ounce) package reduced-fat cream cheese
- ¼ cup confectioners' sugar
- 2 tablespoons frozen orange juice concentrate

1 Preheat the oven to 350°F. Coat a 12-cup muffin tin with cooking spray or line with paper baking cups.

2 In a large bowl, use a wooden spoon to beat the sugar with the margarine until smooth. Stir in the purees, egg, orange juice concentrate, and vanilla, and then the apricots and prunes. Add the flour, baking powder, baking soda, cinnamon, and allspice, and stir until just combined. Do not overmix; there are supposed to be lumps in the batter.

3 Divide the batter among the muffin cups. Bake until the tops of the muffins are lightly browned and a toothpick comes out clean when inserted into the center, 12 to 15 minutes. Turn the muffins out onto a rack to cool.

4 To make the frosting, beat the cream cheese, confectioners' sugar, and orange juice concentrate in a medium bowl until smooth. Spread the frosting on the cooled muffins.

5 Store in an airtight container at room temperature for up to 2 days, or wrap individually and freeze for up to 1 month.

Yellow Cake

(WITH PUMPKIN)

It's a cake from a box, but better for you. Serve as is, or frost with any of the cream cheese frostings in the book.

Prep: 5 minutes • Total: 30 minutes • Makes a 9-inch cake • Packable

- **Nonstick cooking spray**
- **1 (18-ounce) box yellow cake mix (any brand)**
- **1 cup canned pumpkin puree**
- **¼ cup water**
- **2 tablespoons vegetable oil**
- **2 large eggs**
- **1 large egg white**
- **6 ounces nonfat lemon, banana, or vanilla yogurt**

1. Preheat the oven to 350°F. Coat a 9-inch cake pan with cooking spray and flour lightly.

2. In a large mixing bowl or the bowl of an electric mixer, combine the cake mix, pumpkin puree, water, oil, eggs, egg white, and yogurt. Beat until smooth, 1 to 2 minutes.

3. Pour the batter into the cake pan and bake until a toothpick inserted into the cake comes out clean, about 20 minutes.

Variation

DEVIL'S FOOD CAKE:

Substitute a box of devil's food cake mix for the yellow cake mix, and beat with 1 cup pumpkin puree, ¼ cup water, 2 tablespoons canola or vegetable oil, 2 large eggs, 1 large egg white, and ¾ cup plain yogurt (preferably Greek). Bake as above.

Julian: *Can I have this at my birthday party?*

It's About the Celebration, Not the Sugar.

MY ATTITUDE toward birthdays is, admittedly, not one shared by millions, but it seems clear to me that there's too much emphasis on sugar. I watch as my kids navigate their sugar highs and then, of course, crash when they get home. I think a birthday cake is both fine and appropriate, but I've been to children's parties where there are also cookies, candy, and cupcakes served in addition to the cake. If we better understood the effect this has on children's bodies, perhaps we would rethink it. I learned personally from Dr. Roxana Mehran and Dr. Mehmet Oz (who wrote this book's foreword) what really happens to our children's bodies when they eat all this sugar, and it is scary stuff.

Here are a couple of suggestions for scrumptious birthday cakes, fortified with vegetables:

1 Chocolate Cake (page 194)

2 Chocolate Cupcakes (page 172)

3 Yellow cake (page 186)

Also, instead of handing out candy, why not consider giving out little favors (tattoos, shiny rings, bouncy balls), which you can buy in bulk at a party store? They also cost less than buying candy!

Hot Cocoa

(WITH SWEET POTATO)

The familiar taste of chocolate syrup hides the sweet potato puree. It's the puree, though, that makes the cocoa so thick and creamy, even made with skim milk.

Prep: 5 minutes • Total: 6 minutes • Serves 2

- 1¼ cups nonfat (skim) milk
- ½ cup sweet potato puree
- 2 tablespoons chocolate syrup
- ⅛ teaspoon salt
- ⅛ teaspoon cinnamon or pumpkin pie spice (optional)
- Marshmallows, for serving

Combine the milk, sweet potato puree, chocolate syrup, salt, and spice in a blender and blend until smooth. Transfer to a saucepan and bring to a simmer. Pour into mugs and top with marshmallows.

Fruit Punch

(WITH RASPBERRIES, PINEAPPLE, AND CARROT)

It tastes too good to be good for you, but it is!

Prep: 5 minutes • Total: 6 minutes • Serves 4

- 2 cups raspberry puree
- 1 cup pineapple puree
- ½ cup carrot puree
- 2 cups cold water
- ¼ cup sugar
- Ice, for serving

Combine raspberry, pineapple, and carrot purees, water, and sugar in a blender or food processor, and process until smooth. Serve over ice.

Marshmallow Crispy Treats

(WITH BROWN RICE)

Brown rice and flaxseed meal make these traditional favorites better for you.

Total: 10 minutes • Makes 8 large squares • Packable

- **Nonstick cooking spray**
- **1 tablespoon trans-fat-free soft tub margarine spread**
- **1 (10-ounce) package marshmallows**
- **6 cups crisp brown rice cereal**
- **¼ cup flaxseed meal**

1 Coat an 8x8-inch baking pan with cooking spray.

2 Melt the margarine in a large pot over low heat. Add the marshmallows and stir until completely melted. Remove the pan from the heat.

3 Add the rice cereal and flaxseed, and stir until the rice is well coated with marshmallow. Press the mixture into the baking dish and let cool before cutting into squares.

Sascha: *We sell these at the bake sale at school.*

Angel Food Cupcakes

(WITH YELLOW SQUASH AND CARROT)

These are sooo light and airy. I often don't bother with the frosting because they are divine as is, but a shake of confectioners' sugar makes a pretty finish.

Prep: 15 minutes • Total: 35 minutes • Makes 12 cupcakes • Packable

- **5 large egg whites**
- **³⁄₄ teaspoon cream of tartar**
- **¹⁄₄ teaspoon salt**
- **¹⁄₂ cup all-purpose flour**
- **¹⁄₂ cup sugar**
- **¹⁄₄ cup yellow squash puree**
- **1 teaspoon pure lemon extract**
- **1 teaspoon grated lemon or orange zest**

FROSTING (OPTIONAL)

- **1 (8-ounce) package reduced-fat cream cheese**
- **¹⁄₂ cup carrot puree**
- **2 tablespoons frozen orange juice concentrate**
- **¹⁄₈ teaspoon salt**

1 Preheat the oven to 350°F. Line a 12-cup muffin tin with paper baking cups.

2 In the bowl of an electric mixer, combine the egg whites, cream of tartar, and salt. Beat until the egg whites double in volume and stiff peaks form, 4 to 5 minutes. Add the flour, sugar, squash puree, lemon extract, and zest; using a rubber spatula, gently fold these ingredients into the egg whites just until combined.

3 Divide the batter among the muffin cups and bake until the tops of the cupcakes are lightly browned and spring back to the touch, 18 to 20 minutes. Turn the cupcakes out onto a rack to cool.

4 For the frosting, beat the cream cheese, carrot puree, orange juice concentrate, and salt in a medium bowl until smooth. Spread the frosting over the cooled cupcakes.

5 Store in an airtight container at room temperature for up to 2 days, or wrap individually and freeze for up to 1 month.

Chocolate Cake

(WITH BEETS)

A scrumptious, traditional chocolate cake that just happens to be fortified with beets. A fabulous alternative to the usual birthday cake!

Prep: 15 minutes • Total: 55 minutes • Makes a 9-inch cake

BATTER
- Nonstick cooking spray
- 1 cup firmly packed light or dark brown sugar
- ¼ cup canola or vegetable oil, or trans-fat-free soft tub margarine spread
- 1 large egg
- 2 large egg whites
- 3 ounces semisweet or bittersweet chocolate, melted and cooled
- ½ cup beet puree
- ½ cup lowfat (1%) buttermilk
- 1 teaspoon pure vanilla extract
- 2 cups all-purpose flour
- 1 teaspoon baking soda
- ¼ teaspoon salt

CREAM CHEESE FROSTING
- 1 (8-ounce) package reduced-fat cream cheese
- ¾ cup confectioners' sugar
- ½ cup unsweetened cocoa powder
- 1 tablespoon pure vanilla extract

1 Preheat the oven to 350°F. Coat a 9-inch baking pan with cooking spray.

2 In a large mixing bowl or the bowl of an electric mixer, beat the brown sugar with the oil or margarine until creamy. Add the whole egg and egg whites one at a time, beating well after each addition. Beat in the melted chocolate, beet puree, buttermilk, and vanilla.

3 Add the flour, baking soda, and salt, and beat until smooth.

4 Pour the batter into the pan and bake until a toothpick comes out clean when inserted into the center, 35 to 40 minutes. Let the cake cool 5 minutes in the pan before turning it out onto a rack to cool completely.

5 Meanwhile, make the frosting. Beat the cream cheese with the confectioners' sugar, cocoa powder, and vanilla until smooth. Slice the cake in half horizontally. Spread the frosting over the top and between the layers of the cooled cake.

6 Refrigerate in an airtight container for up to 4 days.

Oatmeal Raisin Cookies

(WITH BANANA AND ZUCCHINI)

Jerry's favorite. Don't use an electric mixer—it will make the cookies tough.

Prep: 20 minutes • Total: 35 minutes • Makes 2 dozen cookies

- **Nonstick cooking spray**
- **1 cup whole-wheat flour**
- **1 cup old-fashioned oats**
- **1 teaspoon baking soda**
- **½ teaspoon salt**
- **¼ teaspoon cinnamon**
- **¾ cup firmly packed light or dark brown sugar**
- **6 tablespoons trans-fat-free soft tub margarine spread, chilled**
- **½ cup banana puree**
- **½ cup zucchini puree**
- **1 large egg white**
- **½ cup raisins**
- **½ cup chopped walnuts (optional)**

1 Preheat the oven to 350°F. Coat two baking sheets with cooking spray, or line with cooking parchment.

2 In a bowl or zipper-lock bag, combine the flour, oats, baking soda, salt, and cinnamon, and shake or stir to mix.

3 In a large bowl, beat the sugar and margarine with a wooden spoon until just combined; do not overmix. Add the banana and zucchini purees, and the egg white, and stir just to blend. Add the flour mixture, raisins, and walnuts, if using, and stir to combine.

4 Drop the dough by heaping tablespoonsful onto the baking sheets, leaving about 1 inch in between. Bake until golden brown, 12 to 15 minutes. Let the cookies cool on the baking sheets for 4 to 5 minutes, just until they are firm enough to handle, then transfer to a rack to cool completely.

Jerry: *Once Jessica thought she heard a raccoon in the house in the middle of the night. It was me, eating these cookies.*

Chocolate Chip Muffins

(WITH PRUNES OR DATES)

These make a yummy afternoon or after-school snack.

Prep: 10 minutes • Total: 35 minutes • Makes 12 muffins • Packable

- **Nonstick cooking spray**
- **¼ cup prunes or dates**
- **½ cup firmly packed light or dark brown sugar**
- **4 tablespoons trans-fat-free soft tub margarine spread**
- **¾ cup lowfat (1%) buttermilk**
- **¾ cup semisweet chocolate chips**
- **1 large egg white**
- **2 teaspoons pure vanilla extract**
- **2 cups whole-wheat pastry flour or all-purpose flour**
- **1 teaspoon baking powder**
- **1 teaspoon baking soda**
- **½ teaspoon salt**
- **¼ cup toasted wheat germ**

1 Preheat the oven to 350°F. Coat a 12-cup muffin tin with cooking spray or line with paper baking cups.

2 Put the prunes or dates in a blender or mini-chopper with ¼ cup hot water and puree until smooth.

3 In a large mixing bowl, beat the brown sugar and margarine with a wooden spoon until creamy. Stir in the buttermilk, chocolate chips, prune or date puree, egg white, and vanilla.

4 Add the flour, baking powder, baking soda, and salt, and stir until just combined; do not overmix. There should be some lumps in the batter.

5 Divide the batter among the muffin cups. Sprinkle the tops with wheat germ. Bake until the tops of the muffins are lightly browned and a toothpick comes out clean when inserted into the center, 20 to 25 minutes. Turn the muffins out onto a rack to cool.

6 Store in an airtight container at room temperature for up to 2 days, or wrap individually and freeze for up to 1 month.

Save Time

SHORTCUTS are not only okay, they're necessary!

1 If I'm very short on time, I'll often use canned or frozen veggies; check the label to make sure there is no sugar or other additives.

2 Pre-chopped veggies are more expensive but great for purees (I prefer fresh for crudités). Use them as soon as possible after purchase; the shelf life of cut-up vegetables is significantly shorter than for whole veggies.

3 Purees can just as well be added to store-bought foods such as macaroni and cheese and boxed cake mixes. I'd recommend adding the puree incrementally, tasting after each addition, so that you can judge the correct balance of flavor for your family.

Banana Pudding Pie

(WITH CANTALOUPE AND YELLOW SQUASH)

This dessert is a big hit with both kids and adults. I love to serve it frozen—it's a great way to end a weekend brunch.

Prep: 20 minutes • Total: 75 minutes (3 hours if refrigerated) • Serves 8

- 2 (3-ounce) packages instant banana pudding mix
- 1½ cups cantaloupe puree
- ½ cup yellow squash puree
- ¼ cup water
- 1 large banana, thinly sliced (about ½ cup), plus one more, sliced for garnish
- 1 (9-inch) store-bought graham cracker crust (Arrowhead Mills makes a healthier version)
- ½ pint fresh raspberries
- 8 sprigs fresh mint (optional)

1 In a large bowl, combine the pudding mix, cantaloupe and squash purees, and water, and stir with a wooden spoon until smooth.

2 Spread the banana slices in a single layer over the bottom of the piecrust. Pour the pudding mixture over the bananas and smooth the top. Cover and chill until firm, about 3 hours, or freeze 1½ hours.

3 Just before serving, decorate with raspberries, banana slices, and mint sprigs, if you like.

Joy: *Thanks to raspberries and sneaky cantaloupe puree, one serving of this decadent dessert provides nice amounts of vitamin C, beta carotene, and fiber.*

THE ABCs OF EATING WELL

Vitamins

Vitamins are chemical substances that the body needs in very small amounts in order to grow and to run efficiently. We get vitamins from eating both plants and animals. If we don't eat enough (or eat too many) vitamins, the body can become ill.

VITAMIN A is important for healthy eyesight and night vision. It helps in the growth of healthy bones and teeth, and in the development of healthy skin. (It's best to get your Vitamin A in the form of beta carotene—a nutrient found in bright orange and green vegetables which our body converts to Vitamin A as needed.) Good sources of Vitamin A (in the form of beta carotene) are:

- Orange vegetables such as carrots, sweet potatoes, butternut squash, pumpkin, and apricot
- Dark green leafy vegetables

Daily Recommendations
- 1 to 3 years old: 300 mcg/1000 IU
- 4 to 8 years old: 400 mcg/1333 IU
- 9 to 13 years old: 600 mcg/2000 IU

VITAMIN B6 is important for making hormones, enzymes, and hemoglobin (red blood cells) in the blood. It also helps to make antibodies and insulin, and helps to maintain normal brain function. Good sources are:

- Fortified cereals
- Legumes
- Vegetables
- Bananas
- Eggs
- Meat (beef, pork, and chicken)

Daily Recommendations
- Infant to 3 years old: 0.5 mg
- 4 to 8 years old: 0.6 mg
- 9 to 13 years old: 1 mg

VITAMIN B12 helps to make hemoglobin (red blood cells) and helps maintain healthy nerve cells. It is also needed to make DNA, the genetic material found in all cells. Good sources are:
- Fish
- Shellfish
- Meats
- Dairy products

Daily Recommendations
- Infant to 3 years old: 0.9 mcg
- 4 to 8 years old: 1.2 mcg
- 9 to 13 years old: 1.8 mcg

FOLIC ACID is necessary for the normal growth and maintenance of all cells. It also helps to make red blood cells and DNA. Folic acid is found in:

- Dark green leafy vegetables
- Avocados
- Beets
- Broccoli
- Orange juice
- Strawberries

Daily Recommendations

- 1 to 3 years old: 150 mcg
- 4 to 8 years old: 200 mcg
- 9 to 13 years old: 300 mcg

VITAMIN C helps children resist infections by supporting immune cell functions. It also helps make collagen and maintain body tissues, and helps cuts and wounds heal. Good sources of Vitamin C are:

- Red, green, and yellow bell peppers
- Strawberries
- Oranges and grapefruits
- Broccoli
- Brussels sprouts

Daily Recommendations

- 1 to 3 years old: 15 mg
- 4 to 8 years old: 25 mg
- 9 to 13 years old: 45 mg

VITAMIN D helps absorb calcium and is needed for strong bones and teeth. Good sources are:

- Milk
- Wild salmon (fresh or canned), sardines, and other fatty fish
- Egg yolks
- Vitamin D–fortified foods

Daily Recommendations

- Children and adolescents need 5 mcg

VITAMIN E is an antioxidant, which means it helps protect healthy cells from damage. It is also important for healthy red blood cells. Good sources are:

- Vegetable oils
- Avocados
- Nuts
- Seeds
- Wheat germ
- Vitamin E–fortified foods

Daily Recommendations

- Infant to 3 years old: 6 mg
- 4 to 8 years old: 7 mg
- 9 to 13 years old: 11 mg

VITAMIN K is best known for helping blood clot properly after an injury. Good sources of Vitamin K are:

- Turnip greens
- Broccoli
- Kale
- Spinach
- Cabbage
- Asparagus
- Dark green lettuce

Daily Recommendations

- Infant to 3 years old: 30 mcg
- 4 to 8 years old: 55 mcg
- 9 to 13 years old: 60 mcg

Minerals

Two of the most important minerals for kids are iron and calcium—potassium is another one to keep an eye on.

IRON is key for transporting oxygen. If your child is a meat eater (beef, pork, poultry, shellfish, and eggs), you're set. Iron from animal sources (called heme iron) is better absorbed than that from plants (called non-heme iron). If your child isn't a big meat-eater, she or he can consume enough iron from beans, nuts, seeds, fortified cereals, and even raisins and spinach. To help increase the absorption of iron, add Vitamin C to a meal (i.g. bell peppers, tomatoes and tomato sauce, potatoes, strawberries, broccoli, and citrus fruits).

Daily Recommendations
* 1 to 3 year olds: 7 mg
* 4 to 8 year olds: 10 mg
* 9 to 13 year olds: 8 mg

CALCIUM is key for bone health, but it also helps keep muscles working optimally and regulate blood pressure.

Daily Recommendations
* 1 to 3 year olds: 500 mg
* 4 to 8 year olds: 800 mg
* 9 to 18 year olds: 1300 mg

POTASSIUM regulates blood pressure and plays an important role in overall heart health.

MAGNESIUM helps regulate blood sugar levels and is important for overall heart health.

Antioxidants

Antioxidants include *many* different chemical substances, such as vitamins C and E, the mineral selenium, and carotenoids (the most famous carotenoid is beta-carotene, found in butternut squash and carrots, which the body converts to vitamin A). Antioxidants appear to be important for a number of different reasons—they help prevent harmful substances called "free radicals" from damaging healthy cells in the body. Therefore, they have been shown to be helpful in preventing cancer, for example, and heart disease.

INDEX

Aloha Chicken Kebabs, 95
  with sweet potato and pineap-
    ple puree
Alphabet Soup, Chicken, 103
  with cauliflower and sweet
    potato puree
Angel Food Cupcakes, 193
  with summer squash and
    carrot puree
Apple puree, 30
Apples
  nutritional value of, 40
  preparation of, 30
Applesauce Muffins, with butter-
  nut squash and carrot
  puree, 50
Artichokes, Greek Dip with, 123
Avocado puree, 28
  Avocado Spread with, 134
  Chocolate Cupcakes with, 172
  Chocolate Fondue with, 174
  Chocolate Pudding with, 159
Avocado Spread, 136
  with avocado puree
Avocados
  nutritional value of, 37
  preparation of, 28

Baked Egg Puffs, 67
  with summer squash or
    butternut squash puree
Bakeware, 21
  baking sheets, 21
  cake pan, 21
  pie plate, 9-inch, 21
Baking
  dishes, 21
  equipment for, 21
  ingredients needed for, 23
  sheets, 21
Banana Bread, 54
  with cauliflower puree
Banana Pudding Pie, 201
  with summer squash and
    cataloupe puree
Banana puree, 30
  Banana-Marshmallow Dip with,
    163
  French Toast with, 49
  Oatmeal Raisin Cookies with, 197
  Peanut Butter and Banana
    Muffins with, 58
Banana-Marshmallow Dip, with
  butternut squash and
    banana puree, 163
Bananas
  nutritional value of, 40
  preparation of, 30
Beef puree, 31
Beef Stew, 83
  with broccoli puree
Beet puree, 28

Chicken Nuggets with, 75
Chocolate Cake with, 194
Lemon Raspberry Cupcakes
  with, 181
Pink Pancakes with, 143
Beets
  nutritional value of, 37
  preparation of, 28
Beverages
  Fruit Punch, 189
  Hot Cocoa, 189
Blueberries
  nutritional value of, 40
  preparation of, 30
Blueberry Cheesecake Cupcakes,
  with summer squash, spinach,
    and blueberry puree, 178
Blueberry Oatmeal Bars, 171
  with spinach puree
Blueberry puree, 30
  Blueberry Cheesecake Cupcakes
    with, 178
  Yogurt Pops, Frozen with, 167
Blueberry Lemon Muffins, 65
  with summer squash puree
Bowls, mixing, 21
Box grater, 20
Bread, Banana, 54
Broccoli
  nutritional value of, 37
  preparation of, 28
Broccoli puree, 28
  Beef Stew with, 83
  Chicken Nuggets with, 75
  Gingerbread Spice Cake with,
    168
  Rice Balls with, 87
  Spaghetti Pie with, 116
Brown rice
  Marshmallow Crispy Treats
    with, 190
Brownies, 156
  with carrot and spinach puree
Burgers, 111
  with mushrooms and zucchini
    puree, 115
Buttered Noodles, 108
  with summer squash puree
Butternut squash
  nutritional value of, 37
  preparation of, 28
Butternut squash puree, 28
  Applesauce Muffins with, 50
  Baked Egg Puffs with, 67
  Banana-Marshmallow Dip
    with, 163
  Coffee Cake with, 47
  Creamy Potato Soup with, 128
  French Toast with, 49
  Grilled Cheese Sandwiches
    with, 135
  Macaroni and Cheese 1 with,
    103
  Quesadillas with, 124

Rice Balls with, 87
Sloppy Joes with, 147
Spaghetti and Meatballs with,
  120
Tacos with, 148

Cake
  Chocolate, 194
  Coffee, 161
  Gingerbread Spice, 168
  Yellow, 186
Cake pan, 21
Calcium
  nutritional guidelines of, 35
  serving size of, 35
Cantaloupe
  nutritional value of, 40
  preparation of, 30
Cantaloupe puree, 30
  Banana Pudding Pie with,
    201
Carrot Cake Muffins, 185
  with carrot and cauliflower
    puree
Carrot puree, 28
  Angel Food Cupcakes with,
    193
  Applesauce Muffins with, 50
  Brownies with, 156
  Carrot Cake Muffins with,
    185
  Chocolate Fondue with, 174
  Chocolate Peanut Butter Dip
    with, 163
  Couscous with, 152
  Creamy Potato Soup with, 128
  Deviled Eggs with, 99
  French Toast with, 49
  Gingerbread Spice Cake with,
    168
  Hamburgers with, 111
  Fruit Punch with, 189
  Italian Meatloaf with, 79
  Ketchup, homemade, with, 92
  Meatball Soup with, 72
  Peanut Butter and Banana
    Muffins with, 58
  Peanut Butter and Jelly
    Muffins, 63
  Salsa Dip with, 127
  Spaghetti and Meatballs with,
    120
  Spaghetti Pie with, 116
  Tacos with, 148
  Tortilla "Cigars" with, 144
  Turkey Chili with, 151
Carrots
  nutritional value of, 38
  preparation of, 28
Cauliflower
  nutritional value of, 38
  preparation of, 28

Cauliflower puree, 28
  Banana Bread with, 54
  Carrot Cake Muffins with, 185
  Chicken Alphabet Soup with,
    103
  Chicken Salad with, 84
  Chocolate Cupcakes with, 172
  Creamy Potato Soup with, 128
  Deviled Eggs with, 99
  Hamburgers with, 111
  Lasagna with, 131
  Macaroni and Cheese 1, 104
  Mashed Potatoes with, 80
  Mozzarella Sticks with, 91
  Peanut Butter and Banana
    Muffins with, 58
  Scrambled Eggs with, 53
  Tuna Salad and, 112
  Twice-Baked Potatoes with,
    139
Cheese
  Grilled, Sandwiches, 135
Cherries
  nutritional value of, 40
  preparation of, 30
  Cherry puree, 30
Chicken Alphabet Soup, 103
  with cauliflower and sweet
    potato puree
Chicken Kebabs, Aloha, 95
  with sweet potato and
    pineapple puree
Chicken Nuggets, 75
  with broccoli, spinach, sweet
    potato or beet puree
Chicken puree, 31
Chicken Salad, 84
  with cauliflower puree
Chickpeas
  Chocolate Chip Cookies with,
    177
  Greek Dip with, 123
Children
  eating concerns for, 8, 12, 187
  eating habits of, 13, 77, 81, 89,
    93, 106, 118, 126, 141, 153,
    173
  eating schedule for, 81
  nutritional guidelines of,
    34–36
  snacks for, 106, 118, 133
  table rules for, 126
  vegetable views of, 10, 45, 59,
    173
Chili, Turkey, 151
  with red bell pepper and
    carrot puree
Chocolate Cake, 194
  with beet puree
Chocolate Chip Cookies, 177
  with chickpeas
Chocolate Chip Cupcakes, with
  pumpkin and summer squash
    puree, 164

Chocolate Chip Muffins, with prunes or dates, 198
Chocolate Cupcakes, with avocado and cauliflower puree, 172
Chocolate Fondue, with avocado and carrot puree, 174
Chocolate Pudding, 159
  with avocado puree
Chocolate Peanut Butter Dip, with carrot puree, 163
Coffee Cake, 47
  with butternut squash puree
Cookies
  Chocolate Chip, 177
  Oatmeal Raisin, 197
Cookware, 18–21
  12-inch nonstick skillet, 20
  cutting board, 19
  Cooling rack, 21
Couscous, with summer squash and carrot puree, 152
Creamy Potato Soup, 128
  with butternut squash or carrot and cauliflower puree
Cupcakes
  Angel Food, 193
  Blueberry Cheesecake, 178
  Chocolate, 172
  Chocolate Chip, 164
  Lemon Raspberry, 181
Cutting board, 19

Dates, Chocolate Chip Muffins with, 198
Deviled Eggs, 99
  with cauliflower or carrot puree
Dips
  Avocado Spread, 136
  Banana-Marshmallow, 163
  Chocolate Fondue, 174
  Chocolate-Peanut Butter, 163
  Greek, 123
  Ketchup, homemade, 92
  Ranch Dressing, 123
  Salsa, 127
Doughnuts, 160
  with pumpkin and sweet potato puree

Eating habits, of children, 13, 77, 81, 93, 106, 118, 126, 141, 153, 173
Egg Puffs, baked, 67
  with summer squash or butternut squash puree
Eggs, Deviled, 99
  with cauliflower or carrot puree
Eggs, Green, with spinach puree, 62
Eggs, Scrambled, 53
  with cauliflower puree
Electric mixer, 21

Fats
  monounsaturated, 36
  Omega-3, 36
Fiber, 36
Fondue
  Chocolate, 174
Food processor, 18
French toast, 49
  with banana and pineapple puree
Frozen Yogurt Pops, 167
  with mixed berry puree
Fruit Punch, with raspberry, pineapple and carrot puree, 189
Fruits
  importance of, 8–9
  nutritional guidelines of, 34
  puree preparation of, 24, 30
  serving size of, 34

Gingerbread Spice Cake, 168
  with broccoli and carrot puree
Graham Cracker Ice Cream Sandwiches, 182
Grains. See also Whole grains
  stocking of, 22
Grater, box, 20
Greek Dip, 123
  with chickpeas and artichokes
Green Eggs, with spinach puree, 62
Grilled Cheese Sandwiches, 135
  with sweet potato or butternut squash puree

Hamburgers, 111, 115. See also Burgers
  with cauliflower or carrot puree, 111
Healthy meals, steps for, 16
Heart disease, national diet and, 8
Hot Cocoa, 189
  with sweet potato puree
Hummus. See Chickpeas

Ice Cream Sandwiches, Graham Cracker, 182
Ice cream scoop, 21
Italian Meatloaf, 79
  with carrot puree, 77

Kebabs, Aloha Chicken, 95
Ketchup, homemade, with carrot puree, 92
Kitchen
  equipment for, 18–21
  ingredients needed in, 22–23
Lasagna, 131
  with sweet potato and cauliflower puree
Lemon Raspberry Cupcakes, 181
  with summer squash and beet puree
Loaf pan, 9x5, 20

Macaroni and Cheese 1, 104
  with butternut squash or cauliflower puree
Macaroni and Cheese 2, with beans, canned, 107
Marshmallow Crispy Treats, 190
  with brown rice
Mashed Potatoes, with cauliflower puree, 80
Masher, potato, 20
Meat. See Beef; Burgers; Hamburgers
Meatball Soup, 72
  with carrot and sweet potato puree
Meatloaf, Italian, 79
  with carrot puree
Microwaving
  vegetables, 26
Mixed berry puree. See Blueberry puree; Cherry puree; Raspberry puree; Strawberry puree
Mixer, electrical, 21
Mixing bowls, 21
Monounsaturated fats, 36
Mozzarella Sticks, 91
  with cauliflower puree
Muffin pan
  12 cup, 21
  mini, 21
Muffins
  Applesauce, 50
  Blueberry Lemon, 65
  Carrot Cake, 185
  Chocolate Chip, 198
  Peanut Butter and Banana, 58
  Peanut Butter and Jelly, 63
Mushrooms, Burgers with, 115

National diet, heart disease and, 8
Nonstick skillet, 20
Noodles, Buttered, 108
  with summer squash puree
  children's guidelines for, 34–36
  importance of, 10–12
  parent's knowledge of, 32–33
Nutritional value
  of apples, 40
  of avocado, 37
  of bananas, 40
  of beets, 37
  of blueberries, 40
  of broccoli, 37
  of butternut squash, 37
  of cantaloupe, 40
  of carrots, 38
  of cauliflower, 38
  of cherries, 40
  of pineapple, 41
  of pumpkin, 38
  of raspberries, 41
  of red bell pepper, 38
  of spinach, 39
  of strawberries, 41
  of summer squash, 39
  of sweet potato, 39
  of zucchini, 39

Oatmeal, 68
  with pumpkin puree
  Raisin Cookies, 197
  with zucchini and banana puree
Omega-3 fats, 36

Pancakes, 57
  with sweet potato puree
Pancakes, Pink, 143
  with beet puree
Pantry, ingredients needed in, 22–23
Pasta, 31
Pasta with Bolognese Sauce, with sweet potato puree, 119
Peanut Butter and Banana Muffins, with carrot or cauliflower and banana puree, 58
Peanut Butter and Jelly Muffins, with carrot puree, 63
Pie
  Banana Pudding, 201
  plate, 9-inch, 21
  Spaghetti, 116
Pineapple
  nutritional value of, 41
  preparation of, 30
  Pineapple puree, 30
  Aloha Chicken Kebabs with, 95
  French Toast with, 49
  Fruit Punch with, 189
Pink Pancakes, 143
  with beet puree, 141
Pita Pizzas, 96
  with spinach puree, 94
Pizzas, Pita, 96
  with spinach puree, 94
Popsicle mold, 20
Potato masher, 20
Potatoes, Mashed, with cauliflower puree, 80
Potatoes, Twice-Baked, 139
  with cauliflower puree, 137
Pots
  6-quarts, 19
  8-quarts, 19
Preparation
  of apples, 30
  of avocados, 28
  of bananas, 30
  of beets, 28
  of broccoli, 28
  of butternut squash, 28
  of cantaloupe, 30
  of carrots, 28
  of cauliflower, 28
  of cherries, 30
  of mixed berries, 30
  of pineapple, 30
  of purees, 24
  of red bell peppers, 29
  of spinach, 29
  of summer squash, 29
  of sweet potatoes, 29
  of vegetables/fruits, 24
  of zucchini, 29
Protein
  nutritional guidelines of, 35–36

serving size of, 36
Prunes, Chocolate Chip Muffins
    with, 198
Pudding, Chocolate, 159
    with avocado puree, 157
Pumpkin, nutritional value of, 38
Pumpkin puree
    Chocolate Chip Cupcakes
        with, 164
    Doughnuts with, 160
    French Toast with, 49
    Oatmeal with, 68
    Yellow Cake with, 186
Punch, Fruit, with raspberry,
    pineapple and carrot puree,
    189
Purees, 24
    apple, 30
    avocado, 28, 136, 159, 172, 174
    banana, 30, 49, 58, 163, 197
    beef, 31
    beet, 28, 75, 143, 181, 194
    blueberry, 30, 167, 178
    broccoli, 28, 75, 83, 87, 116,
        166
    butternut squash, 28, 50, 67,
        104, 120, 124, 128, 135,
        147, 148, 163
    cantaloupe, 30, 201
    carrot, 28, 50, 63, 72, 79, 92,
        99, 111, 116, 120, 127, 128,
        144, 148, 151, 152, 156,
        163, 168, 174, 185, 189, 193
    cauliflower, 28, 53, 54, 80, 84,
        91, 99, 103, 104, 111, 112,
        128, 131–132, 139, 172
    cherry, 30
    chicken, 31
    equipment for, 18–19
    of fruit, 30
    how to, 24, 25, 26–27
    pineapple, 30, 49, 95, 189
    portion/packaging of, 27
    preparation of, 18
    pumpkin, 49, 68, 160, 164, 186
    raspberry, 30, 167, 189
    red bell pepper, 29, 125, 147,
        151
    spinach, 29, 62, 75, 87, 96,
        100, 156, 171, 178
    strawberry, 30, 167
    sweet potato, 29, 57, 72, 75,
        87, 95, 103, 119, 131, 135,
        140, 147, 148, 160, 189
    time needed for, 24
    vegetable/fruit preparation
        for, 24
    yellow squash, 29, 65, 67, 108,
        144, 152, 164, 178, 181,
        193, 201
    zucchini, 29, 115, 197

Quesadillas, 124
    with butternut squash puree

Rack, cooling, 21
Ranch Dressing, 123
    with beans

Raspberries
    nutritional value of, 41
    preparation of, 30
Raspberry puree, 30
    Fruit Punch with, 189
    Yogurt Pops, Frozen, with,
        167
Red bell pepper puree, 29
    Salsa Dip with, 127
    Sloppy Joes with, 147
    Turkey Chili with, 151
Red bell peppers
    nutritional value of, 38
    preparation of, 29
Rice
    brown, 190
    rice cooker method of, 31
    stovetop method of, 31
Rice Balls, 87
    with sweet potato and
        spinach, broccoli or butter-
        nut squash puree
Roasting
    beets, 28
    butternut squash, 28
    sweet potatoes, 29
    vegetables, 26

Salad
    Chicken, 84
    Tuna, 112
Salsa Dip, with red bell pepper
    or carrot puree, 127
Sandwiches
    Graham Cracker Ice Cream,
        182
    Grilled Cheese, 135
    Waffle, 140
Saucepans
    1-quart, 19
    2-quart, 19
Scissors, 20
Scrambled Eggs, 53
    with cauliflower puree
Serving size, 34
    of calcium, 35
    of fruits, 34
    of protein, 35
    of vegetables, 34
    of whole grains, 34
Sheets, baking, 21
Skillet, nonstick, 20
Sloppy Joes, 147
    with butternut squash or red
        bell pepper and sweet
        potato puree
Soup
    Chicken Alphabet, 103
    Creamy Potato, 128
    Meatball, 72
Spaghetti and Meatballs, 120
    with butternut squash and
        carrot puree
Spaghetti Pie, 116
    with broccoli and carrot puree
Spatula, heatproof silicone, 21
Spices, stocking of, 22
Spinach
    nutritional value of, 39
    preparation of, 29

Spinach puree, 29
    Blueberry Cheesecake
        Cupcakes with, 178
    Blueberry Oatmeal Bars with,
        169
    Brownies with, 156
    Chicken Nuggets with, 75
    Green Eggs with, 62
    Pita Pizza with, 96
    Rice Balls with, 87
    Tofu Nuggets with, 100
Spoon, wooden, 19
Squash. See Butternut squash;
    Yellow Squash
Steamers, 18
Steaming
    broccoli, 28
    butternut squash, 28
    carrots, 28
    cauliflower, 28
    red bell peppers, 29
    spinach, 29
    summer squash, 29
    sweet potatoes, 29
    vegetables, 26
    zucchini, 29
Strawberries
    nutritional value of, 41
    preparation of, 30
Strawberry puree, 30
    Yogurt Pops, Frozen, with,
        167
Summer Squash, see Yellow
    Squash
Sweet potato puree, 29
    Aloha Chicken Kebabs with,
        95
    Chicken Alphabet Soup with,
        103
    Chicken Nuggets with, 75
    Doughnuts with, 160
    French Toast with, 49
    Grilled Cheese Sandwiches
        with, 135
    Hot Cocoa with, 189
    Lasagna with, 131
    Meatball Soup with, 72
    Pancakes with, 57
    Pasta with Bolognese Sauce
        with, 119
    Rice Balls with, 87
    Sloppy Joes with, 147
    Tacos with, 148
    Waffle Sandwiches with, 140
Sweet potatoes
    nutritional value of, 39
    preparation of, 29

Tacos, 148
    with sweet potato, carrot or
        butternut squash puree
Tofu Nuggets, 100
    with spinach puree
Tortilla "Cigars," 144
    with summer squash and car-
        rot puree
Tuna Salad, 112
    with cauliflower puree
Turkey Chili, 151
    with red bell pepper and

carrot puree
Twice-Baked Potatoes, 139
    with cauliflower puree

Utensils
    heatproof silicone spatula, 21
    ice cream scoop, 21
    potato masher, 20
    scissors, 20
    whisk, 21
    wooden spoon, 19

Vegetables
    cooking of, 26
    importance of, 8–9, 33
    nutritional guidelines of, 34
    puree preparation of, 24, 28
    roasting/steaming/microwav-
        ing, 26
    serving size of, 34

Waffle Sandwiches, with sweet
    potato puree, 140
Whisk, 21
Whole grains
    nutritional guidelines of,
        34–35
    serving size of, 35
Wooden spoon, 19

Yellow Cake, with pumpkin
    puree, 186
Yellow squash
    nutritional value of, 39
    preparation of, 29
    Summer squash puree, 29
    Angel Food Cupcakes with,
        193
    Baked Egg Puffs with, 67
    Banana Pudding Pie with,
        201
    Blueberry Cheesecake
        Cupcakes with, 178
    Blueberry Lemon Muffins
        with, 65
    Buttered Noodles with, 108
    Chocolate Chip Cupcakes
        with, 164
    Couscous with, 152
    Lemon Raspberry Cupcakes
        with, 181
    Tortilla "Cigars" with, 144
Yogurt Pops, Frozen, with mixed
    berry puree, 167

Zucchini
    nutritional value of, 39
    preparation of, 29
Zucchini puree, 29
    Burgers with, 115
    Oatmeal Raisin Cookies with,
        197

Acknowledgments

I wholeheartedly share credit for this book with those who made it better than I could have ever done myself—Stephanie Lyness, Chef Jennifer Iserloh, Lia Ronnen, Joy Bauer, and Drs. Mehmet Oz and Roxana Mehran. Their contributions to this book are immeasurable and invaluable. Specifically, Stephanie Lyness and her ability to take my work and articulate, organize, and strengthen it made her my lifeline from start to finish. The wonderful Chef Jen worked patiently with me to create and test (endlessly) our recipes so that they are family-friendly, Joy Bauer–approved, and best of all, delicious. As the project manager, Lia Ronnen suffered every detail of this book with me, always with a smile. She, along with Charlie Melcher, art director Paul Kepple of Headcase Design, photographer Lisa Hubbard and illustrator Steve Vance were each masterful in helping to create the look, feel, and beautiful production of this book.

Most important, the evolution of this book starts with Elizabeth Wiatt and Jennifer Rudolph Walsh for their instantaneous belief in this idea. Jane Friedman, Joe Tessitore, Kathryn Huck, and the team at HarperCollins gave this book a very happy home.

Without my family and friends it is impossible to imagine this book happening.

My amazing team at Baby Buggy, headed by Claudia Fleming, helped me step back and focus on recipes and writing for a little while.

Elizabeth Clark Zoia, Tom Keaney, Steven Rubenstein, Ricky Strauss, Rich Ross, Hal Petri, Martha Lebron, Sofija Sefa, Rosie Aquino, Ricardo Souza, Kate Fenneman, Dr. Pat Schimm, Dr. Jean Mandelbaum, and Dr. Barbara Landreth have my endless appreciation for always being tremendously supportive.

Additional thanks to Eric Zohn, Lee Eastman, Cara Stein, and Rachel Nagler.

Ellen Rakieten, Tina Sharkey, Alexandra Wentworth, Ally Lieberman, Rain Kramer, Sarah Easley, Courtney Denaro, Stefani Greenfield, Narciso Rodriguez, Bette Ann and Charles Gwathmey, SJP, and Carolyn Liebling have my deep thanks for their infinite love and friendship.

As always, I want to express my deeper-than-describable love and appreciation to my grandmother, Eleanor Furman, my parents Ellen and Karl Sklar, my sisters Rebecca Shalam and Elzy Wick. To my husband, my love. And to Sascha, Julian, and Shepherd, I hope this book will serve as a reminder of how much I love every inch of you all, inside and out.

Finally, and sadly, I must acknowledge the prescience of Chris Rock, who years ago said to me, "Well, now that you're married to a celebrity, the cookbook is only a matter of time."

—Jessica Seinfeld, 2007